A Guide to Writing

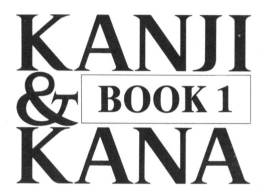

KANJI & KANA

BOOK 1

A SELF-STUDY WORKBOOK FOR LEARNING JAPANESE CHARACTERS

by Wolfgang Hadamitzky and Mark Spahn

Tuttle Publishing
Boston • Rutland, Vermont • Tokyo

Published by Tuttle Publishing
an imprint of Periplus Editions (HK) Ltd.

LCC Card No. 91-65055
ISBN 0-8048-1685-9

First edition, 1991
Twelfth printing, 2001

Printed in Singapore

Distributed by:

Japan & Korea
Tuttle Publishing
RK Building 2nd Floor
2-13-10 Shimo-Meguro, Meguro-ku
Tokyo 153 0064
Tel: (03) 5437 0171
Fax: (03) 5437 0755

North America
Tuttle Publishing
Distribution Center
Airport Industrial Park
364 Innovation Drive
North Clarendon, VT 05759-9436
Tel: (802) 773 8930
Fax: (802) 773 6993

Asia Pacific
Berkeley Books Pte. Ltd.
130 Joo Seng Road
#06-01/03
Olivine Building
Singapore 368357
Tel: (65) 280 1330
Fax: (65) 280 6290

CONTENTS

INTRODUCTION

The purpose of *A Guide to Writing Kanji and Kana* is to help students of Japanese master writing the two *kana* syllabaries (46 hiragana and 46 katakana) and the 1,945 basic characters (Jōyō Kanji) officially recommended for daily use.

With so many characters, it is important that you study them systematically, in a carefully thought-out progression. Most textbooks for learning Japanese, however, do not offer an introduction to Japanese script based on sound didactic principles. *A Guide to Writing Kanji and Kana* answers the need for a step-by-step presentation of characters by following the system developed in the book *Kanji & Kana* [1]. Also, up to three basic graphical elements (graphemes) indicating its meaning and/ or pronunciation are listed for each kanji. Furthermore, the characters are taught not in isolation but as parts of important compounds that use only characters that have been introduced earlier.

Characters are presented in brush, pen, and printed forms. Each character in pen form is printed in light gray for you to trace over. These gray lines will guide your hand the first time you try writing a new character and will help you quickly develop a feel for the proper proportions.

When practicing writing the characters, don't forget that they should be written to fit into squares, either real or imaginary, of exactly the same size. *A Guide to Writing Kanji and Kana* has convenient, preprinted squares: large and normal size for all kana and the first 778 kanji, and normal size for kanji 779–1,945.

The best way to begin learning the Japanese writing system is to start with one of the two syllabaries, either hiragana or katakana. This is because:

1. The number of characters is limited to 46 characters per syllabary.

2. The forms of the characters are simple (there are one to four strokes per kana).

3. Each character has only one pronunciation (except for two characters that have two readings).

4. The kana syllabaries represent the entire phonology of the Japanese language, which means that any text can be written entirely in kana and without using any kanji at all.

---

[1] Hadamitzky, Wolfgang and Mark Spahn: *Kanji & Kana: A Handbook and Dictionary of the Japanese Writing System,* Charles E. Tuttle Company, Rutland, VT and Tokyo, 1981.

It is difficult to say which syllabary should be learned first. If you learn katakana first, even as a beginner you will be able to write many words, especially loanwords from English, that you already know. Hiragana, however, is by far the more widely used syllabary. We recommend the following learning sequence as the quickest way to master hiragana or katakana; for best results, we suggest using, if available, the computer program *SUNRISE Script* [2] to help you learn correct pronunciation.

1. Divide either syllabary into **several small units**. Concentrate on only a few kana at each session. Begin, for instance, with the first five vowels of hiragana.

2. Practice the **pronunciation** of each kana, first while looking at the transcription and later without looking. This will help you link the sound of each kana to its visual image.

3. Memorize the **order of the syllables** (*a-i-u-e-o, ka-ki-ku-ke-ko*) by reading them aloud.

4. Memorize the **shape** of each kana and compare it to that of other kana; take notice of similarities and peculiarities.

5. Memorize the **order** in which the strokes are written and the **direction** in which each stroke is written.

6. **Practice writing** each kana, first writing on the three gray pen forms in the large squares. Practice each kana until you can write it with the correct stroke order, stroke direction, and proportions without looking at the model.

7. Read aloud and **write all the words** that are given as examples for each character. Using *SUNRISE Script*, you can browse through the kana you've learned, manually or automatically, in a given order or at random, at various speeds, and with or without the audio function.

8. After finishing all the characters of either the hiragana or katakana syllabary, **review** them to check your grasp of forms and sounds.

9. **Repeat** the above steps for each unit.

10. **Review regularly**.

When memorizing kanji, use the same method as the one recommended above for the syllabaries. For kanji, look at the **basic graphical elements** (graphemes) the entry character is made up of; you will soon notice that all kanji are constructed from relatively few basic elements. These elements often indicate the meaning and/or pronunciation of the kanji. Instead of following the order of kanji presented in this book, you can choose any order you like. You might, for example, select the order in which kanji are introduced in the textbook you're using in class. The disadvantage to this, however, is that the words and compounds will then contain characters that you have not yet learned.

The kanji are fully indexed by *on-kun* readings. The *Index* in Book 1 lists all kanji contained in that volume. The *General Index* at the end of Book 2 lists all kanji contained in both volumes, grouping together kanji that share the same reading and a common graphical element.

---

[2] Hadamitzky, Wolfgang and Mark Spahn: *SUNRISE Script: Electronic Learning and Reference System for Kanji*, JAPAN Media, Berlin, 1989. (With this computer program you can both hear and read the pronunciation of the characters.)

EXPLANATION OF THE CHARACTER ENTRIES

Hiragana/Katakana

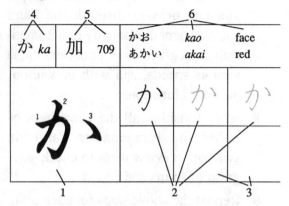

1. The kana character in brush form, with numbers showing stroke order positioned at the beginning of each stroke.

2. Squares with the kana character in pen form, printed in light gray, and serving as a practice template to trace over.

3. Empty squares in which to write first the kana character and then the example words.

4. The kana character in printed form, with pronunciation in roman letters.

5. Kanji from which the kana character is derived, with the sequential number of that kanji.

6. Up to four common words, with romanization and meanings. These words contain only kana that have already been introduced.

Kanji

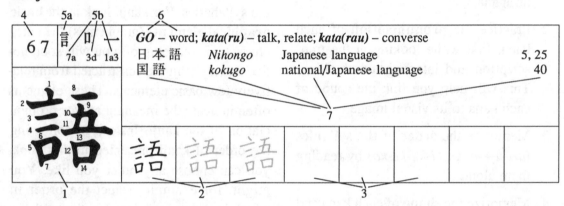

1. The kanji in brush form, with numbers showing stroke order positioned at the beginning of each stroke.

2. Three squares with the kanji in pen form, printed in light gray and serving as a practice template to trace over.

3. Empty squares in which to write the entry kanji and compounds.

4. Number of the kanji in these manuals.

5. a. Radical with its number-and-letter "descriptor", under which the kanji is listed in the *Japanese Character Dictionary*[3].

   b. Up to three graphemes (basic elements) with their number-and-letter "descriptor", under which the kanji can be retrieved in *SUNRISE Script* (see footnote 2).

   A numeral from 2 to 4 added to the descriptor indicates how many times that radical or grapheme is contained in the kanji. If the radical is not a grapheme, it is put in parentheses.

6. *On* readings, in capital italics; *kun* readings, in lowercase italics; readings that are infrequent or used only in special cases, in brackets; *okurigana* (part of a word that is written in kana), in parentheses; English meanings. All officially recognized readings of the kanji are listed.

7. Compounds, with romanization, meanings, and cross-reference numbers to the main entries for other kanji in the compound.

---

[3] Spahn, Mark and Wolfgang Hadamitzky: *Japanese Character Dictionary: With Compound Lookup via Any Kanji*, Nichigai Associates, Tokyo, 1989.

あ	a	安	105	ああ	ā	ah, oh

あ

い	i	以	46	いい	ii	good, alright	あい	ai	love, affection

い

あい　あい

う	u	宇 990	あう	*au*	meet		いう	*iu*	say

う ううう う うう
う ううう う うう

う う う

え	e	衣 677	え うえ	*e* *ue*	picture, painting top, area above	ええ いいえ	*ē* *iie*	yes, yeah, uh-huh no

え え え え え え え え
え え え え え え え え

え え え
え え え え え

お *o* 於 –	あおい	*aoi*	blue, green	おおい	*ōi*	lots of, many

お

お	お	お				
お	お	お	お	お	お	お

| お | お | お | お | お | お | お | | | | | | |

か *ka* 加 709	かお あかい	*kao* *akai*	face red	かう えいが	*kau* *eiga*	buy, purchase movie

か

か	か	か				

| か | か | か | | | | | | | | | | |
| が | が | が | | | | | | | | | | |

き	*ki*	幾	877	あき	*aki*	autumn		えき	*eki*	(train) station
				おおきい	*ōkii*	big, large		かぎ	*kagi*	key

	き	き	き							
	き	き	き	き	き	き	き			

き	き	き	き	き	き								
き	き	き	き	き	き	き	き						
ぎ	ぎ	ぎ	ぎ										

く	*ku*	久	1210	いく	*iku*	go		きく	*kiku*	hear; ask
				かく	*kaku*	write		かぐ	*kagu*	furniture

	く	く	く							
	く	く								

く	く	く											
ぐ	ぐ	ぐ	ぐ	ぐ	ぐ								

け ke	計 340	いけ	*ike*	pond		けいき	*keiki*	times, business	

こ ko	己 370	ここ ごご	*koko* *gogo*	here, this place afternoon	こえ えいご	*koe* *eigo*	voice English (language)

さ *sa*	左	75	さあ さけ	*sā* *sake*	well now, alright saké	あさ けいざい	*asa* *keizai*	morning economy

さ さ さ さ

さ さ さ さ さ

さ さ さ さ さ さ さ

さ さ さ さ さ さ さ さ さ

ざ ざ ざ

し *shi*	之	-	あし おいしい	*ashi* *oishii*	leg, foot tasty, tastes good	いし あじ	*ishi* *aji*	stone taste, savor

し し し

し し し し

し し し

し し し

し し

じ じ じ

す *su*	寸	1894	すし いす	*sushi* *isu*	sushi chair			あす かず	*asu* *kazu*	tomorrow number

せ *se*	世	252	あせ かぜ	*ase* *kaze*	sweat, perspiration wind, breeze	せいじ なぜ	*seiji* *naze*	politics why

そ - た

| そ so | 曽 | – | そう | *sō* | so, like that | そこ | *soko* | there |
| | | | うそ | *uso* | lie, falsehood | かぞく | *kazoku* | family |

そ そ そ

そ そ そ
ぞ ぞ ぞ

| た ta | 太 629 | たかい | *takai* | high; expensive | した | *shita* | bottom, area below |
| | | かた | *kata* | person (polite) | ただしい | *tadashii* | correct |

た た た

た た た

た た た
だ だ だ

14

ち *chi*	知 214	ちいさい いち	*chiisai* *ichi*	little, small one		ちかい うち	*chikai* *uchi*	near home, residence

ち ち ち ち

ち ち ち ち ち ち

ち ち ち ち ち ち ち ち ち

ぢ ぢ ぢ

つ *tsu*	川 33	つぎ いくつ	*tsugi* *ikutsu*	the next how many		つかう がっこう	*tsukau* *gakkō*	use school

つ つ つ

つ つ つ

つ つ つ つ

つ

つ つ つ つ つ つ つ つ つ つ

つ

づ づ づ

| て | *te* | 天 | 141 | て
きって | *te*
kitte | hand
(postage) stamp | ちかてつ
です | *chikatetsu*
desu | subway
be |

て　て　て　て

て　て　て

で　で　で

| と | *to* | 止 | 477 | とおい
せいと | *tōi*
seito | far
pupil, student | とし
いちど | *toshi*
ichido | year; city
one time, once |

と　と　と　と

と　と　と　と　と　と

と　と　と　と　と　と

ど　ど　ど

な na	奈	–	ななつ なか	*nanatsu* *naka*	seven the inside		なつ おなじ	*natsu* *onaji*	summer the same

な　な　な

な　な　な
な　な　な　な　な　な　な　な　な

に ni	仁	1619	にし にど	*nishi* *nido*	west twice, two times		にく なに	*niku* *nani*	meat what

に　に　に　に　に　に
に　に　に　に　に　に

に　に　に

ぬ - ね

ぬ *nu*	奴 1933	ぬぐ しぬ	*nugu* *shinu*	take/peel off die		いぬ きぬ	*inu* *kinu*	dog silk

ね *ne*	祢 -	ねこ おかね	*neko* *okane*	cat money		ねがい あね	*negai* *ane*	a request elder sister

の no	乃	–	ので この	*node* *kono*	because, since this	のど たのしい	*nodo* *tanoshii*	throat merry, pleasant

の

は ha/ wa	波	666	はは (は) にばい	*haha (wa)* *nibai*	mother (wa = particle) double, twice as much	はい しっぱい	*hai* *shippai*	yes failure, flop

は

ば ば ぱ

ぱ ぱ ぱ

ひ hi	比 798	ひと くび	*hito* *kubi*	person, man neck		ひがし いっぴき	*higashi* *ippiki*	east one (animal)

ひ ひ ひ

ひ ひ ひ

ひ ひ ひ ひ ひ ひ

ひ

び び び

ひ び び

ぴ ぴ ぴ ぴ ぴ ぴ

ふ fu	不 94	ふたつ どうぶつ	*futatsu* *dōbutsu*	two animal		ふね きっぷ	*fune* *kippu*	ship ticket

ふ ふ ふ

ぶ ぶ ぶ

ぷ ぷ ぷ

へ he/ e	部 86	へた かべ	*heta* *kabe*	unskillfulness wall			どこへ ぺらぺら	*doko e* *perapera*	where to (speak) fluently		
へ		ヘ	⌒	⌒							
		⌒	⌒	⌒							
⌒	⌒	⌒	⌒	⌒	⌒						
⌒	⌒	⌒	⌒								
べ	べ	べ	べ	へ	べ	へ					
ぺ	ぺ	ぺ	ぺ	ぺ	ぺ	ぺ	ぺ				

ほ ho	保 489	ほか ぼうし	*hoka* *bōshi*	other hat			ほね ぽかぽか	*hone* *pokapoka*	bone repeatedly		
ほ		ほ	ほ	ほ							
		ほ	ほ	ほ	ほ						
ぼ	ぼ	ぼ	ほ	ほ	ぼ	ほ					
ぽ	ぽ	ぽ									

ま *ma*	末	305	まつ しま	*matsu* *shima*	wait island		なまえ いま	*namae* *ima*	name now	

み *mi*	美	401	みみ うみ	*mimi* *umi*	ear sea, ocean		みせ みなみ	*mise* *minami*	shop, store south	

| む mu | 武 1031 | むっつ | *muttsu* | six | | むずかしい | *muzukashii* | difficult |
| | | よむ | *yomu* | read | | さむい | *samui* | cold |

む　む　む

む　む　む

| め me | 女 102 | めいし | *meishi* | name card | | あめ | *ame* | rain |
| | | だめ | *dame* | useless, vain | | いつつめ | *itsutsume* | the fifth |

め　め　め

め　め　め

も mo	毛	287	もの	*mono*	thing, object	もう	*mō*	already
			もじ	*moji*	character, letter	もっと	*motto*	more

も も も

も も も も

と も も も も

も も も も も も
も も も も も

や ya	也	–	やすい	*yasui*	cheap, inexpensive	やさしい	*yasashii*	easy, simple
			やま	*yama*	mountain	ひゃく	*hyaku*	hundred

や や や

や や や

ゆ *yu*	由 363	ゆき ふゆ	*yuki* *fuyu*	snow winter		ゆうめい きゅう	*yūmei* *kyū*	famous nine

ゆ ゆ ゆ

ゆ ゆ ゆ

よ *yo*	与 539	よい よっつ	*yoi* *yottsu*	good, alright four		よむ きょう	*yomu* *kyō*	read today

よ よ よ

よ よ よ よ よ よ よ

よ よ よ

ら *ra*	良	321	から ひらがな	*kara* *hiragana*	from; because hiragana		いくら さようなら	*ikura* *sayōnara*	how much goodbye

ら　ら　ら　ら

ら　ら　ら　ら　ら

ら　ら　ら

ら　ら　ら
ら　ら　ら　ら

り *ri*	利	329	かなり まつり	*kanari* *matsuri*	quite, rather festival		あります りょこう	*arimasu* *ryokō*	be (present) trip, travel

り　り　り　り　り　り　り　り

り　り　り　り　り　り　り　り

る ru	留	761	くる	*kuru*	come		ある	*aru*	be
			よる	*yoru*	(at) night, evening		ふるい	*furui*	old

る る る る

る る る

れ re	礼	620	れい	*rei*	example		これ	*kore*	this
			かれ	*kare*	he		きれい	*kirei*	pretty; clean

れ れ れ れ

れ れ れ

ろ ro	呂	–	ろく しろい	*roku* *shiroi*	six white		いろ ところ	*iro* *tokoro*	color place	

ろ ろ ろ

ろ ろ ろ

わ wa	和	124	わたし わるい	*watashi* *warui*	I bad, evil		わかる にわ には	*wakaru* *niwa ni wa*	understand in the garden	

わ わ わ

わ わ わ

28

を o 遠 446	おちゃ を のむ *ocha o nomu* drink (green) tea しお を かう *shio o kau* buy salt

を

を　を　を

を　を　を

ん n 尤 -	なん *nan* what おんな *onna* woman	よん *yon* four かんぱい *Kanpai!* To your health!

ん

ん　ん　ん　ん　ん　ん

ん　ん　ん　ん

ん　ん　ん　ん　ん

ん　ん　ん

KATAKANA

ア a	阿 –	アー	*aa*	ah, oh					
ア	ア	ア	ア						

ア	ア	ア											

イ i	伊 –	イー	*ii*	good, alright	アイ	*ai*	love, affection		
イ	イ	イ	イ						

イ	イ	イ											

| ウ _u_ 宇 990 | アウ | _au_ | meet | イウ | _iu_ | say |

ウ	ウ	ウ	ウ						

ウ ウ ウ												

| エ _e_ 江 821 | エ
ウエ | _e_
_ue_ | picture, painting
top, area above | エー
イーエ | _ee_
iie | yes, yeah, uh-huh
no |

エ	エ	エ	エ						

エ エ エ												

| オ | *o* | 於 | – | アオイ | *aoi* | blue, green | | オーイ | *ooi* | lots of, many |

| オ | オ | オ | | | | | | | |

| オ | オ | オ | | | | | | | | | | |

| カ | *ka* | 加 | 709 | カー | *kā* | car | | | | |

| カ | カ | カ | | | | | | | |

| カ | カ | カ | | | | | | | | | | |
| ガ | ガ | ガ | | | | | | | | | | |

キ *ki*	幾 877	キー	*kī*	key

キ キ キ

キ キ キ
ギ ギ ギ

ク *ku*	久 1210	アーク	*āku*	(electric) arc

ク ク ク

ク ク ク
グ グ グ

ケ ke	介 453	ケーキ	*kēki*	cake		オーケー	*ōkē*	O.K., okay

ケ	ケ	ケ	ケ						

ケ	ケ	ケ										
ゲ	ゲ	ゲ										

コ ko	己 370	コア	*koa*	core		ゴア	*goa*	Goa

コ	コ	コ	コ						

コ	コ	コ										
ゴ	ゴ	ゴ										

サ *sa*	散 767	サー	*sā*	sir					
サ	サ	サ	サ						

サ	サ	サ												
ザ	ザ	ザ												

シ *shi*	之 －	シガー	*shigā*	cigar		アジア	*ajia*	Asia	
シ	シ	シ	シ						

シ	シ	シ												
ジ	ジ	ジ												

ス *su*	須	–	スキー コース	*sukī* *kōsu*	skiing, skis course		ガス スイス	*gasu* *Suisu*	gas Switzerland	
ス		ス	ス	ス						
ス	ス	ス								
ズ	ズ	ズ								

セ *se*	世	252	セクシー	*sekushī*	sexy		ガーゼ	*gāze*	gauze	
セ		セ	セ	セ						
セ	セ	セ								
ゼ	ゼ	ゼ								

ソ *so*	曽	–	ソース	*sōsu*	sauce		ソーセージ	*sōsēji*	sausage
			ソれん	*Soren*	Soviet Union				

ソ		
ソ	ソ	ソ

ソ	ソ	ソ								
ゾ	ゾ	ゾ								

タ *ta*	多	229	タクシー	*takushī*	taxi		ウエーター	*uētā*	waiter
			ギター	*gitā*	guitar		えいがスター	*eiga sutā*	movie star

タ		
タ	タ	タ

タ	タ	タ								
ダ	ダ	ダ								

チ *chi*	千	15	チーズ	*chīzu*	cheese			チェス	*chesu*	chess	
チ			チ	チ	チ						
チ チ チ											
ヂ ヂ ヂ											

ツ *tsu*	川	33	スーツケース	*sūtsukēsu*	suitcase			クッキー	*kukkī*	cookie	
			サッカー	*sakkā*	soccer			チェック	*chekku*	check	
ツ			ツ	ツ	ツ						
ツ ツ ツ											
ヅ ヅ ヅ											

テ *te* 天 141	データ	*dēta*	data	ディスク	*disuku*	disk
	シーディー	*shīdī*	CD (compact disk)			

テ テ テ テ

テ テ テ
デ デ デ

ト *to* 止 477	テスト	*tesuto*	test	テキスト	*tekisuto*	text
	スカート	*sukāto*	skirt	ドット	*dotto*	dot

ト ト ト

ト ト ト
ド ド ド

ナ *na*	奈	–	ナチ (ス)	*nachi(su)*	the Nazis		カナダ	*Kanada*	Canada

ナ ナ ナ

ナ ナ ナ

ニ *ni*	仁 1619	ニーズ	*nīzu*	needs		テニス	*tenisu*	tennis

二 二 二

二 二 二

ヌ *nu*	奴 1933	ヌード	*nūdo*	nude		カヌー	*kanū*	canoe
ヌ		ヌ	ヌ	ヌ				

ヌ ヌ ヌ

ネ *ne*	祢 -	ネクタイ *nekutai* necktie	ゼネスト *zenesuto* general strike
		ネガ *nega* (photographic) negative	

ネ		ネ	ネ	ネ				

ネ ネ ネ

ノ no	乃	–	ノー	nō	no		ノート	nōto	notebook

ノ

ノ	ノ	ノ						

ノ	ノ	ノ											

ハ ha	八	10	バス	basu	bus		バナナ	banana	banana
			スーパー	sūpā	supermarket		デパート	depāto	department store

ハ

ハ	ハ	ハ						

バ	バ	バ											
パ	パ	パ											

| ヒ hi | 比 798 | コーヒー | *kōhī* | coffee | | ビデオ | *bideo* | video |
| | | サービス | *sābisu* | service | | コピー | *kopī* | copy |

ヒ　ヒ　ヒ　ヒ

ビ ビ ビ

ピ ピ ピ

| フ fu | 不 94 | ナイフ | *naifu* | knife | | ストーブ | *sutōbu* | stove |
| | | コップ | *koppu* | (drinking) glass | | フォーク | *fōku* | fork |

フ　フ　フ　フ

ブ ブ ブ

プ プ プ

へ he	部	86	ベッド	*beddo*	bed			データーベース	*dētābēsu*	database
			ページ	*pēji*	page					

へ	へ	へ	へ							
ベ	ベ	ベ								
ペ	ペ	ペ								

ホ ho	保	489	ホステス	*hosutesu*	hostess			ボーナス	*bōnasu*	bonus
			ポスト	*posuto*	post(box)			スポーツ	*supōtsu*	sports

ホ	ホ	ホ	ホ							
ボ	ボ	ボ								
ポ	ポ	ポ								

マ *ma*	末 305	ママ テーマ	*mama* *tēma*	mama theme			パーマ マーケット	*pāma* *māketto*	permanent (wave) market
マ		マ	マ	マ					
マ マ マ									

ミ *mi*	三 4	ミニカー マスコミ	*minikā* *masukomi*	minicar mass communication			ミス ゼミ	*misu* *zemi*	mistake; Miss seminar
ミ		ミ	ミ	ミ					
ミ ミ ミ									

ム mu	牟	–	ゲーム	*gēmu*	game		ブーム	*būmu*	boom
			ハム	*hamu*	ham		けしゴム	*keshigomu*	eraser

ム	ム	ム								
ム	ム	ム								

メ me	女	102	メーデー	*mēdē*	May Day		メッセージ	*messēji*	message
			メキシコ	*Mekishiko*	Mexiko		メッカ	*Mekka*	Mecca

メ	メ	メ								
メ	メ	メ								

モ mo	毛 287	モーター メモ	*mōtā* *memo*	motor memo, note, list	モットー デモ	*mottō* *demo*	motto demonstration

モ モ モ

モ モ モ

ヤ ya	也 −	カヤック シャツ	*kayakku* *shatsu*	kayak undershirt	ジャズ キャベツ	*jazu* *kyabetsu*	jazz cabbage

ヤ ヤ ヤ

ヤ ヤ ヤ

ユ *yu*	由	363	ユニーク	*yunīku*	unique			ユーモア	*yūmoa*	humor	
			ニュース	*nyūsu*	news			メニュー	*menyū*	menu	

ユ

ユ ユ ユ

ユ ユ ユ

ヨ *yo*	與	–	ヨット	*yotto*	yacht		ニューヨーク	*Nyū Yōku*	New York
			ショー	*shō*	show				

ヨ

ヨ ヨ ヨ

ヨ ヨ ヨ

ラ *ra*	良 321	ラジオ	*rajio*	radio		カメラ	*kamera*	camera
		カラー	*karā*	color		グラム	*guramu*	gram

ラ	ラ	ラ	ラ									
ラ	ラ	ラ										

リ *ri*	利 329	リズム	*rizumu*	rhythm		リスト	*risuto*	list
		ミリ	*miri*	millimeter		ベーカリー	*bēkarī*	bakery

リ	リ	リ	リ									
リ	リ	リ										

ル *ru*	流 247	ビル ホテル	*biru* *hoteru*	building hotel		ビール ドル	*bīru* *doru*	beer dollar	

ル ル ル

ル ル ル

レ *re*	礼 620	レコード トイレ	*rekōdo* *toire*	record toilet		ステレオ *sutereo* stereo エレベーター *erebētā* elevator			

レ レ レ

レ レ レ

| ロ *ro* | 呂 | – | ロビー | *robī* | lobby | | ローマじ | *rōmaji* | roman letters | |
| | | | ロシア | *Roshia* | Russia | | ゼロ | *zero* | zero | |

| ワ *wa* | 和 | 124 | ワープロ | *wāpuro* | word processor | | ワイシャツ | *waishatsu* | shirt | |
| | | | タワー | *tawā* | tower | | シャワー | *shawā* | shower | |

ヲ *o* 乎 _		シャワー ヲ アビル *shawā o abiru* take a shower						
ヲ	ヲ	ヲ	ヲ					
ヲ ヲ ヲ								

ン *n* 尓 _		センター *sentā* center パーセント *pāsento* percent				ワイン *wain* wine コンピュータ *konpyūta* computer		
ン	ン	ン	ン					
ン ン ン								

1	イ 2a

JIN, NIN, hito – human being, man, person

アメリカ人	*Amerikajin*	an American
100人	*hyakunin*	100 people
5，6人	*gorokunin*	5 or 6 people
あの人	*ano hito*	that person, he, she
人々	*hitobito*	people

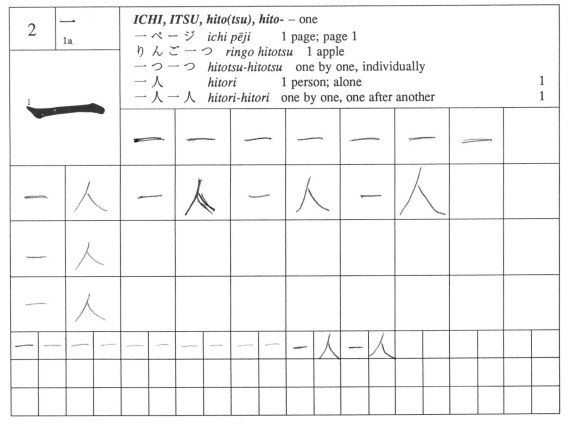

2	一 1a

ICHI, ITSU, hito(tsu), hito- – one

一ページ	*ichi pēji*	1 page; page 1	
りんご一つ	*ringo hitotsu*	1 apple	
一つ一つ	*hitotsu-hitotsu*	one by one, individually	
一人	*hitori*	1 person; alone	1
一人一人	*hitori-hitori*	one by one, one after another	1

3	一 1a2	**NI, futa(tsu), futa** – two

二人　　　　*futari, ninin*　2 people　　　　　　　　　　　　1
一人二人　　*hitori futari*　1 or 2 people　　　　　　　　2, 1
二人ずつ　　*futarizutsu*　two by two, every 2 people　　1
二人とも　　*futaritomo*　both people, both (of them)　　1
二けた　　　*futaketa*　2 digits; 2-digit, double-digit

4	一 1a3	**SAN, mit(tsu), mi(tsu), mi** – three

三人　　　　　　*sannin*　　　3 people　　　　　　　　　1
二, 三人　　　　*nisannin*　　2 or 3 people　　　　　　3, 1
三キロ　　　　　*sankiro*　　　3 kg; 3 km
三つぞろい　　　*mitsuzoroi*　3-piece suit
二つ三つ　　　　*futatsu mittsu*　2 or 3　　　　　　　　3

5	日 4c	**NICHI, JITSU, hi, -ka** – day; sun			
		一日	*ichinichi, ichijitsu*	1 day	2
			tsuitachi	1st of the month	
		二日	*futsuka*	2 days; 2nd of the month	3
		三日	*mikka*	3 days; 3rd of the month	4
		二, 三日	*nisannichi*	2 or 3 days	3, 4

6	口 丶丶 3s 2o	**SHI, yot(tsu), yo(tsu), yo, yon** – four			
		四人	*yonin*	4 people	1
		四日	*yokka*	4 days; 4th of the month	5
		三, 四日	*san'yokka*	3 or 4 days	4, 5
		三, 四人	*san'yonin*	3 or 4 people	4, 1
		四つんばい	*yotsunbai*	(on) all fours	

7 一ノ 1a3 1c	***GO, itsu(tsu), itsu* – five**			
	五人	*gonin*	5 people	1
	五日	*itsuka*	5 days; 5th of the month	5
	四, 五日	*shigonichi*	4 or 5 days	6, 5
	四, 五人	*shigonin*	4 or 5 people	6, 1
	三々五々	*sansan-gogo*	in small groups, by twos and threes	4

五　　五　　五　　五　　五　　五　　五

五 五 五 五 五 五 五 五 五 五 五 五 五

8 六ソ 2j 2o	***ROKU, mut(tsu), mu(tsu), mu, [mui]* – six**			
	六人	*rokunin*	6 people	1
	五, 六人	*gorokunin*	5 or 6 people	7, 1
	六日	*muika*	6 days; 6th of the month	5
	五, 六日	*gorokunichi*	5 or 6 days	7, 5
	六つぐらい	*muttsu-gurai*	about 6	

六　　六　　六　　六　　六　　六　　六

六 六 六 六 六 六 六 六

9	｜ ノ 1b 1c	***SHICHI, nana(tsu), nana, [nano]*** – seven

七人　　　*shichinin*　　7 people　　　　　　　　　　　　　　　　1
七日　　　*nanoka*　　　7 days; 7th of the month　　　　　　　　5
七メートル　*nanamētoru, shichimētoru*　7 meters
七五三　　*Shichigosan*　festival day for 3-, 5-, and 7-year-olds
　　　　　　　　　　　　　　(Nov. 15)　　　　　　　　　　　　7, 4

10	＼＼ 2o	***HACHI, yat(tsu), ya(tsu), ya, [yō]*** – eight

八人　　　*hachinin*　　8 people　　　　　　　　　　　　　　　　1
八日　　　*yōka*　　　　8 days; 8th of the month　　　　　　　　5
八ミリ　　*hachimiri*　　8 mm
八グラム　*hachiguramu*　8 grams
お八つ　　*oyatsu*　　　afternoon snack

11	一 丨 1a 1b	**KYŪ, KU, kokono(tsu), kokono** – nine

九 人 　　kyūnin　　9 people　　　　　　　　　　1
九 日 　　kokonoka　9 days; 9th of the month　　5
九 ド ル　kyūdoru　　9 dollars
九 九 　　kuku　　　multiplication table

九 九 九 九 九 九 九 九

九 九 九

九 九 九 九 九 九 九 九 九 九

12	十 2k	**JŪ, JI', tō, to** – ten

十 人 　　　jūnin　　　　10 people　　　　　　　　　　1
十 日 　　　tōka　　　　10 days; 10th of the month　　5
二 十 日　　hatsuka　　　20 days; 20th of the month　　3, 5
十 四 日　　jūyokka　　　14 days; 14th of the month　　6, 5
十 八 日　　jūhachinichi　18 days; 18th of the month　10, 5

十 十 十 十 十 十 十 十

十 十 十 十 十 十 十

13	冂 一 丨	***EN*** – circle; yen; ***maru(i)*** – round						
	2r 1a 1b	一 円 *ichien* 1 yen 2						
		二 円 *nien* 2 yen 3						
		三 円 *san'en* 3 yen 4						
		四 円 *yoen* 4 yen 6						
		十 円 *jūen, tōen* 10 yen 12						

14	日 一 ノ	***HYAKU*** – hundred						
	4c 1a 1c	百 人 *hyakunin* 100 people 1						
		三 百 六 十 五 日 *sanbyaku rokujūgonichi* 365 days 4, 8, 12, 7, 5						
		八 百 円 *happyakuen* 800 yen 10, 13						
		九 百 *kyūhyaku* 900 11						

15	十 ノ 2k 1c	**SEN, chi** – thousand		
		一千	*issen*	1,000	2
		三千	*sanzen*	3,000	4
		八千	*hassen*	8,000	10
		千円	*sen'en*	1,000 yen	13
		千人	*sennin*	1,000 people	1

千　千　千

千　千　千

16	一 ノ 1a2 1c	**MAN** – ten thousand; **BAN** – many, all		
		一万円	*ichiman'en*	10,000 yen	2, 13
		百万	*hyakuman*	1 million	14
		一千万円	*issenman'en*	10 million yen	2, 15, 13
		二,三万円	*nisanman'en*	20,000-30,000 yen	3, 4, 13
		万一	*man'ichi*	by any chance, should happen to	2

万　万　万

万　万　万

17	月 4b	***GETSU, tsuki*** – moon; month; ***GATSU*** – month

一 月　　　*ichigatsu*　　January　　　　　　　　　　2
　　　　　　hitotsuki　　1 month
一 か 月　　*ikkagetsu*　　1 month　　　　　　　　　　2
一 月 八 日　*ichigatsu yōka*　January 8　　　　　　2, 10, 5
月 ロ ケ ッ ト　*tsuki roketto*　moon rocket

月　月　月

月　月　月

18	日 月 4c 4b	***MEI*** – light; ***MYŌ*** – light; next; ***a(kari)*** – light, clearness; ***aka(rui)*** – bright; ***aki(raka)*** – clear; ***a(keru), aka(rumu/ramu)*** – become light; ***a(ku)*** – be open; ***a(kasu)*** – pass (the night); divulge; ***a(kuru)*** – next, following

明 日　　　*myōnichi, asu*　tomorrow　　　　　　　　5
明 く る 日　*akuruhi*　　　the next/following day　　　5

明　明　明

明　明　明

19	日 隹 一 4c 8c 1a6	**YŌ** – day of the week

曜 日	yōbi	day of the week	5
日 曜（日）	nichiyō(bi)	Sunday	5
月 曜（日）	getsuyō(bi)	Monday	17, 5

曜　曜　曜

曜　曜　曜

20	火 4d	**KA, hi, [ho]** – fire

| 火 曜（日） | kayō(bi) | Tuesday | 19, 5 |
| 九 月 四 日（火） | kugatsu yokka (ka) | (Tuesday) September 4 | 11, 6, 17, 5 |

火　火　火

火　火　火

21	氵 3a	***SUI, mizu*** – water	
		水曜 (日) *suiyō(bi)* Wednesday 19, 5	
		水がめ *mizugame* water jug/jar	
		水かさ *mizukasa* volume of water (of a river)	

水　水　水

水　水　水

22	木 4a	***BOKU, MOKU, ki, [ko]*** – tree, wood	
		木曜 (日) *mokuyō(bi)* Thursday 19, 5	
		木こり *kikori* woodcutter, lumberjack, logger	
		木々 *kigi* every tree; many trees	
		千木 *chigi* ornamental crossbeams on a Shinto shrine 15	
		三木 *Miki* (surname) 4	

木　木　木

木　木　木

23	金 8a	**KIN, KON** – gold; metal; money; **kane** – money; **[kana]** – metal

金曜（日）　*kin'yō(bi)*　　Friday　　　　　　　　　19, 5
金メダル　*kinmedaru*　　gold medal
金ぱく　　*kinpaku*　　　gold leaf/foil
金もうけ　*kanemōke*　　making money

金　金　金

金　金　金

24	土 3b	**DO, TO, tsuchi** – earth, soil, ground

土曜（日）　*doyō(bi)*　　Saturday　　　　　　　　19, 5
土木　　　*doboku*　　　civil engineering　　　　　22
土人　　　*dojin*　　　　native, aborigine　　　　　1
土のう　　*donō*　　　　sandbag

土　土　土　土　土

土　土　土

25	一 木 1a 4a

HON – book; origin; main; this; (counter of long, thin objects); *moto* – origin

日本	*Nihon, Nippon*	Japan	5
日本人	*Nihonjin, Nipponjin*	a Japanese	5, 1
本日	*honjitsu*	today	5
本土	*hondo*	mainland	24
ビール六本	*bīru roppon*	6 bottles of beer	8

26	一 亻 1a 2a

DAI, TAI, ō(kii), ō- – big, large; **ō(i ni)** – very much, greatly

大金	*taikin*	large amount of money	23
大きさ	*ōkisa*	size	
大水	*ōmizu*	flooding, overflow	21
大みそか	*Ōmisoka*	New Year's Eve	
大人	*otona*	adult	1

27	`` 3n	***SHŌ, chii(sai), ko-, o-*** – little, small			
		小人	*kobito*	dwarf, midget	1
			shōjin	insignificant person; small-minded man	
			shōnin	child	
		大小	*daishō*	large and small; size	26
		小金	*kogane*	small sum of money; small fortune	23

小　小　小

小 小 小

28	丨口 1b　3s	***CHŪ, naka*** – middle; inside; throughout			
		日本中	*Nipponjū, Nihonjū*	all over Japan	5, 25
		一日中	*ichinichijū*	all day long	2, 5
		日中	*nitchū*	during the daytime	5
			Nit-Chū	Japanese-Chinese, Sino-Japanese	
		中小	*chūshō*	medium and small; smaller, minor	27

中　中　中

中 中 中

29

几 虫 ノ
2s 6d 1c

FŪ, [FU] – wind; appearance; style; **kaze, [kaza]** – wind

日本風	nihonfū	Japanese-style	5, 25
風土	fūdo	natural features, climate	24
中風	chūfū, chūbu, chūbū	paralysis, palsy	28
そよ風	soyokaze	gentle breeze	

30

雫
8d

U, ame, [ama] – rain

風雨	fūu	wind and rain	29
大雨	ōame	heavy rain, downpour	26
小雨	kosame	light/fine rain	27
にわか雨	niwakaame	sudden shower	
雨水	amamizu	rainwater	21

| 31 | ト 一
2m 1a | **KA, GE, shita, moto** – lower, base; **shimo** – lower part; **sa(geru), o(rosu), kuda(su)** – lower, hand down (a verdict); **sa(garu)** – hang down, fall; **o(riru)** – get out of/off (a vehicle); **kuda(ru)** – go/come down; **kuda(saru)** – give |

| 下水 | *gesui* | sewer system, drainage | 21 |
| 風下 | *kazashimo* | leeward side | 29 |

下　下　下

下　下　下

| 32 | ト 一
2m 1a | **JŌ, [SHŌ], ue** – upper; **kami, [uwa-]** – upper part; **a(geru)** – raise; **a(garu), nobo(ru)** – rise; **nobo(seru/su)** – bring up (a topic) |

水上	*suijō*	on the water	21
上下	*jōge*	high and low, rise and fall	31
上り下り	*noborikudari*	ascent and descent, ups and downs	31

上　上　上

上　上　上

33	I 1b3	**SEN, kawa** – river

川上　　kawakami　upstream　32
川下　　kawashimo　downstream　31
小川　　ogawa　stream, brook, creek　27
ミシシッピー川　Mishishippī-gawa　Mississippi River
中川　　Nakagawa　(surname)　28

川

34	山 3o	**SAN, yama** – mountain

山水　　sansui　landscape, natural scenery　21
火山　　kazan　volcano　20
下山　　gezan　descent from a mountain　31
小山　　koyama　hill　27
山々　　yamayama　mountains

山

35	田 5f	**DEN, ta** – rice field, paddy			
		水 田	*suiden*	rice paddy	21
		田 中	*Tanaka*	(surname)	28
		本 田	*Honda*	(surname)	25
		山 田	*Yamada*	(surname)	34
		下 田	*Shimoda*	(city on Izu Peninsula)	31

36	火 田 4d 5f	**hata, hatake** – cultivated field		
		田 畑	*tahata*	fields	35
		みかん畑	*mikan-batake*	mandarin orange/tangerine orchard	

分

37	刂 2f	**TŌ, katana** – sword, knife									

日本刀　　*nihontō*　　Japanese sword　　5, 25
大刀　　　*daitō*　　long sword　　26
小刀　　　*shōtō*　　short sword　　27
　　　　　kogatana　knife, pocketknife
山刀　　　*yamagatana*　woodsman's hatchet　　34

刀	刀	刀	刀	刀	刀	刀					
刀	刀	刀									

38	゛ 刂 2o 2f	**BUN** – portion; **BU** – portion, 1 percent; **FUN** – minute (of time/arc); **wa(keru/katsu)** – divide, share, distinguish; **wa(kareru)** – be separated; **wa(karu)** – understand									

十分　　　*jūbun*　　enough, sufficient, adequate (cf. No. 828)　　12
　　　　　jippun　　10 minutes
水分　　　*suibun*　　water content　　21

分	分	分	分	分							
分	分	分									

39	刂 一 丨	***SETSU, [SAI], ki(ru)*** – cut; ***ki(reru)*** – cut well; break off; run out of	
	2f 1a 1b	大切 *taisetsu* important; precious	26
		一切れ *hitokire* slice, piece	2
		切り上げ *kiriage* conclusion; rounding up; revaluation	32
		切り下げ *kirisage* reduction; devaluation	31

切

40	口王 丶	***KOKU, kuni*** – country	
	3s 4f 1d	大国 *taikoku* large/great country, major power	26
		万国 *bankoku* all countries, world	16
		六か国 *rokkakoku* 6 countries	8
		四国 *Shikoku* (one of the 4 main islands of Japan)	6
		中国 *Chūgoku* China; (region in western Honshu)	28

国

41	土 十 、		***JI, tera*** – temple		
	3b 2k 1d		国分寺　*Kokubunji*　(common temple name)　　40, 38		
			山寺　　*yamadera*　mountain temple　　　　　　34		

寺　寺　寺

寺　寺　寺

42	日 土 十		***JI, toki*** – time; hour
	4c 3b 2k		四時二十分 *yoji nijippun*　4:20　　　　6, 3, 12, 38

一 時　　*ichiji*　　　　for a time; 1 o'clock　　　2
　　　　　hitotoki, ittoki　a while, moment
時 々　　*tokidoki*　　　sometimes
日 時　　*nichiji*　　　　time, date, day and hour　　5

時　時　時

時　時　時

43	門日 8e 4c	**KAN, KEN, aida** – interval (between); **ma** – interval (between); a room

時 間	jikan	time; hour	42
中 間	chūkan	middle, intermediate	28
人 間	ningen	human being	1
間 も な く	mamonaku	presently, in a little while, soon	

間　間　間

間　間　間

44	一土ノ 1a 3b 1c	**SEI, SHŌ** – life; **i(kiru/keru)** – be alive; **i(kasu)** – revive, bring to life; let live; **u(mu)** – bear (a child); **u(mareru)** – be born; **ha(yasu/eru), o(u)** – grow; **nama** – raw, draft (beer); **ki-** – pure

人 生	jinsei	(human) life	1
一 生	isshō	one's whole life	2
生 ビ ー ル	namabīru	draft beer	

生　生　生

生　生　生

45	一 十 丨 1a2 2k 1b	**NEN, toshi** – year								
年		生年月日 *seinengappi* date of birth							44, 17, 5	
		１９９１年 *sen kyūhyaku kyūjūichinen* 1991								
		五年間 *gonenkan* for 5 years							7, 43	
		年金 *nenkin* pension, annuity							23	
		三年生 *sannensei* third-year student, junior							4, 44	
		年	年	年						
年	年	年								

46	丨 亻 ノ 1b 2a 1c	**I** – (prefix)								
以		以上 *ijō* or more; more than; above-mentioned							32	
		三時間以上 *sanjikan ijō* at least 3 hours							4, 42, 43, 32	
		以下 *ika* or less; less than; as follows							31	
		三つ以下 *mittsu ika* 3 or fewer							4, 31	
		以	以	以						
以	以	以								

47	`ヽ 月 刂` 2o 4b 2f	**ZEN, mae** – before, in front of; earlier		
前		以 前　　　*izen*　　　　　　ago, previously, formerly		46
		前もって　*maemotte*　　　beforehand, in advance		
		人前(で)　*hitomae (de)*　before others, in public		1
		分け前　　*wakemae*　　　　one's share		38
		二人前　　*nininmae, futarimae*　enough for 2 people		3, 1

48	`彳 夂 ノ` 3i 4i 1c2	**GO, nochi** – after, later; **KŌ, ushi(ro)** – behind; **ato** – afterward, subsequent; back, retro-; **oku(reru)** – be late, lag behind		
後		以 後　　　*igo*　　　　　　　hereafter; since then		46
		前 後　　　*zengo*　　　　　approximately; front and rear		47
		明後日　　*myōgonichi, asatte*　day after tomorrow		18, 5
		その後　　*sonogo*　　　　　thereafter, later		

49	十 一 ノ	***GO*** – noon

	2k	1a	1c

午

午 前	*gozen*	A.M.	47
午 後	*gogo*	afternoon; P.M.	48
午 前 中	*gozenchū*	all morning, before noon	47, 28
午 前 も 午 後 も	*gozen mo gogo mo*	both morning and afternoon	47, 48
午 後 四 時	*gogo yoji*	4:00 P.M.	6, 48, 42

午 午 午

午 午 午

50	土 ゛ ノ	***SEN, saki*** – earlier; ahead; priority; future; destination; the tip

	3b	2o	1c

先

先 日	*senjitsu*	recently, the other day	5
先 月	*sengetsu*	last month	17
先 々 月	*sensengetsu*	month before last	17
先 生	*sensei*	teacher	44

先 先 先

先 先 先

51	イ 一 2a 1a2	*KON, KIN, ima* – now

今日　　konnichi, kyō　today　　　　　　　　　5
今月　　kongetsu　this month　　　　　　　17
今年　　kotoshi　this year　　　　　　　　　45
今後　　kongo　after this, from now on　　48
今ごろ　imagoro　about this time (of day)

今　今　今

今　今　今

52	ノ 、 1c 1d	*NYŪ, hai(ru), i(ru)* – go/come/get in, enter; *i(reru)* – put/let in

入国　　　nyūkoku　entry into a country　　40
金入れ　　kaneire　cashbox; purse, wallet　23
日の入り　hi no iri　sunset　　　　　　　　　5
入り日　　irihi　setting sun　　　　　　　　　5

入　入　入

入　入　入

53	丨 山 1b2 3o	**SHUTSU, [SUI], da(su)** – take out; send; **de(ru)** – go/come out		
		出火	shukka	outbreak of fire	20
		出入り	deiri	coming and going (of people)	52
		人出	hitode	turnout, crowds	1
		日の出	hi no de	sunrise	5

54	口 3d	**KŌ, KU, kuchi** – mouth		
		人口	jinkō	population, number of inhabitants	1
		入(り)口	iriguchi	entrance	52
		出口	deguchi	exit	53
		川口	kawaguchi	mouth of a river	33
		口出し	kuchidashi	meddling, butting in	53

55	目 5c	*MOKU, [BOKU], me, [ma]* – eye; (suffix for ordinals)								
		一目	*ichimoku, hitome*	a glance						2
		人目	*hitome*	notice, public attention						1
		目上	*meue*	one's superior/senior						32
		目下	*meshita*	one's subordinate/junior						31
			mokka	at present						

56	耳 6e	*JI, mimi* – ear								
		耳目	*jimoku*	eye and ear; attention; notice						55
		中耳	*chūji*	the middle ear						28
		耳たぶ	*mimitabu*	earlobe						

57	扌 3c

SHU, te, [ta] – hand

切手	kitte	(postage) stamp	39
小切手	kogitte	(bank) check	27, 39
手本	tehon	model, example, pattern	25
上手	jōzu	skilled, good (at)	32
下手	heta	unskilled, poor (at)	31

58	足 7d

SOKU, ashi – foot, leg; **ta(ru/riru)** – be enough, sufficient; **ta(su)** – add up, add (to)

一足	issoku	1 pair (of shoes/socks)	2
	hitoashi	a step	
手足	teashi	hands and feet, limbs	57
足下に	ashimoto ni	at one's feet; (watch your) step	31

59	一 丨 ノ 1a4 1b1 1c2

SHIN, *mi* – body

身上	*shinjō*	strong point, merit; personal background	32
	shinshō	one's fortune; property	
出身	*-shusshin*	(be) from ...	53
前身	*zenshin*	one's past life; predecessor	47
身分	*mibun*	one's social standing; identity	38

身　身　身

身　身　身

60	亻 木 2a 4a

KYŪ, *yasu(mu)* – rest; *yasu(meru)* – give it a rest; *yasu(maru)* – be rested

休日	*kyūjitsu*	holiday, day off	5
一休み	*hitoyasumi*	short rest	2
中休み	*nakayasumi*	a break, recess	28
休み中	*yasumichū*	Closed (shop sign)	28

休　休　休

休　休　休

61	イ 木 一 2a 4a 1a	**_TAI, TEI, karada_** – body			
		身体	_shintai_	body	59
		人体	_jintai_	the human body	1
		五体	_gotai_	the whole body	7
		大体	_daitai_	gist; on the whole, generally	26
		風体	_fūtei, fūtai_	(outward) appearance	29

62	目 ノ 5c 1c	**_JI, SHI, mizuka(ra)_** – self			
		自分	_jibun_	oneself, one's own	38
		自身	_jishin_	oneself, itself	59
		自体	_jitai_	one's own body; itself	61
		自国	_jikoku_	one's own country	40
		自らの手で	_mizukara no te de_	with one's own hands	57

63	目 丷 5c 2o	**KEN, mi(ru)** – see; **mi(eru)** – be visible; **mi(seru)** – show

一 見　　　ikken　　　(quick) glance　　　2
先 見　　　senken　　　foresight　　　50
見 本　　　mihon　　　sample (of merchandise)　　　25
見 出 し　midashi　　heading, headline　　　53
見 分 け る　miwakeru　tell apart, recognize　　　38

見　見　見

見　見　見

64	門 耳 8e 6e	**BUN, MON, ki(ku)** – hear; heed; ask; **ki(koeru)** – be audible

見 聞　　　　kenbun　　　information, observation, experience　　　63
風 聞　　　　fūbun　　　hearsay, rumor　　　29
聞 き 手　　kikite　　　listener　　　57
聞 き 入 れ る　kikiireru　accede to, comply with　　　52

聞　聞　聞

聞　聞　聞

65	耳 又 6e 2h	**SHU, to(ru)** – take

取り出す　*toridasu*　take out; pick out　　53
取り上げる　*toriageru*　take up; adopt; take away　　32
聞き取る　*kikitoru*　catch, follow (what someone says)　　64
日取り　*hidori*　appointed day　　5
足取り　*ashidori*　way of walking, gait　　58

66	言 7a	**GEN, GON, -koto** – word; **i(u)** – say

一言　　　*ichigon, hitokoto*　a word, brief comment　　2
一言二言　*hitokoto futakoto*　a word or two　　2, 3
言明　　　*genmei*　declaration, definite statement　　18
小言　　　*kogoto*　a scolding; complaints, griping　　27
言い分　　*iibun*　one's say; objection　　38

67	言 口 一 7a 3d 1a3	**GO** – word; **kata(ru)** – talk, relate; **kata(rau)** – converse		
語		日本語 *Nihongo* Japanese language		5, 25
		国語 *kokugo* national/Japanese language		40
		言語 *gengo* speech, language		66
		一語一語 *ichigo-ichigo* word for word, verbatim		2
		語り手 *katarite* narrator, storyteller		57

語	語	語							

語	語	語							

68	彳 一 丨 3i 1a2 1b	**KŌ, [AN], i(ku), yu(ku)** – go; **GYŌ** – line (of text); **okona(u)** – do, perform, carry out		
行		一行 *ikkō* party, retinue		2
		ichigyō a line (of text)		
		行間 *gyōkan* space between lines (of text)		43
		行き先 *ikisaki, yukisaki* destination		50

行	行	行							

行	行	行							

69	一米 1a 6b	***RAI, ku(ru), kita(ru)*** – come; ***kita(su)*** – bring about		
		来年	*rainen*	next year	45
		来月	*raigetsu*	next month	17
		来日	*rainichi*	come to Japan	5
		本来	*honrai*	originally, primarily	25
		以来	*irai*	(ever) since	46

70	方 4h	***HŌ*** – direction, side; ***kata*** – direction; person; method		
		一方	*ippō*	on the other hand; only	2
		四方	*shihō*	north, south, east, west; all directions	6
		八方	*happō*	all directions, all sides	10
		方言	*hōgen*	dialect	66
		目方	*mekata*	weight	55

71	一 木 日 (1a) 4a 4c	**TŌ, higashi** – east			

東方　　　*tōhō*　　　the eastward, east　　　70
中東　　　*Chūtō*　　　Middle East　　　28
東大　　　*Tōdai*　　　University of Tokyo
　　　　　　　　　　　(abbrev. for 東京大学 *Tōkyō Daigaku*)　26
東アジア　*Higashi Ajia*　East Asia

72	一 口 ゛ 1a 3s 2o	**SEI, SAI, nishi** – west			

西方　　　　*seihō*　　　　the westward, west　　　70
東西　　　　*tōzai*　　　　east and west　　　71
西風　　　　*seifū, nishikaze*　westerly wind　　　29
西日　　　　*nishibi*　　　the afternoon sun　　　5
西ヨーロッパ　*Nishi Yōroppa*　Western Europe

73	一 卜 丨 1a 2m 1b	***HOKU, kita*** – north

北

北方	*hoppō*	the northward, north	70
北風	*hokufū, kitakaze*	wind from the north	29
東北	*Tōhoku*	(region in northern Honshu)	71
北東	*hokutō*	northeast	71
北北東	*hokuhokutō*	north-northeast	71

北　北　北

北　北　北

74	十 冂 丷 2k2 2r 2o	***NAN, [NA], minami*** – south

南

西南	*seinan*	southwest	72
東南アジア	*Tōnan Ajia*	Southeast Asia	71
南北	*nanboku*	south and north, north-south	73
南アルプス	*Minami Arupusu*	Southern (Japan) Alps	
南口	*minamiguchi*	southern entrance/exit	54

南　南　南

南　南　南

75	一 厂 丨 1a2 2p 1b	**SA, hidari** – left			
		左方	sahō	left side	70
		左手	hidarite	left hand; (on) the left	57
		左足	hidariashi	left foot/leg	58
		左目	hidarime	left eye	55
		左上	hidariue	upper left	32

左　左　左

左　左　左

76	口 厂 3d 2p	**U, YŪ, migi** – right			
		右方	uhō	right side	70
		左右	sayū	left and right; control	75
		右手	migite	right hand; (on) the right	57
		右足	migiashi	right foot/leg	58
		右から左へ	migi kara hidari e	from right to left; quickly	75

右　右　右

右　右　右

77	⼩一 3n 1a3	**TŌ, a(teru/taru)** – hit, be on target

当

本当　　　hontō　　　truth; really　　　　　　　　　　　　　　　25
当時　　　tōji　　　　at present; at that time　　　　　　　　42
当分　　　tōbun　　　for now, for a while　　　　　　　　　　38
手当て　　teate　　　　allowance, compensation; medical treatment　57
一人当たり hitoriatari　per person, per capita　　　　　　　　2, 1

78	石 5a	**SEKI, [SHAKU], ishi** – stone; **[KOKU]** – (unit of volume, about 180 liters)

石

石けん　　sekken　　　soap
木石　　　bokuseki　　trees and stones; inanimate objects　　22
小石　　　koishi　　　small stone, pebble　　　　　　　　　27
石切り　　ishikiri　　　stonecutting, quarrying　　　　　　　39

79	牛 一 ノ 4g 1a 1c3	**BUTSU, MOTSU, mono** – object, thing		
		人 物	*jinbutsu*	person, personage	1
		生 物	*seibutsu*	living beings, life	44
		見 物	*kenbutsu*	sightseeing	63
		物 語	*monogatari*	tale, story	67
		本 物	*honmono*	genuine, the real thing	25

物

物　物　物

物 物 物

80	一 口 十 1a3 3s 2k	**JI, [ZU], koto** – thing, affair		
		人 事	*jinji*	human/personnel affairs	1
		火 事	*kaji*	a fire	20
		事 前/後	*jizen/go*	before/after the fact	47, 48
		大 事	*daiji*	great thing, important	26
		出 来 事	*dekigoto*	event, occurrence	53, 69

事

事　事　事

事 事 事

81	`、` `ク`	***SEKI, yū*** – evening			
	1d 2n	一 夕	*isseki*	one evening	2
		夕 方	*yūgata*	evening	70
		夕 日	*yūhi*	evening/setting sun	5
		夕 月	*yūzuki*	evening moon	17
		七 夕	*tanabata*	Star Festival (July 7)	9

82	`口` `ク` `、`	***MEI, MYŌ, na*** – name, reputation			
	3d 2n 1d	人 名	*jinmei*	name of person	1
		名 人	*meijin*	master, expert, virtuoso	1
		名 物	*meibutsu*	noted product (of a locality)	79
		大 名	*daimyō*	(Japanese) feudal lord	26
		名 前	*namae*	a name	47

83	ト ク 丶 2m 2n 1d	**GAI, GE, soto** – outside; **hoka** – other; **hazu(reru/su)** – slip off; miss

外 (国) 人　　*gai(koku)jin*　foreigner　　　　　　　　　　40, 1
外来語　　　*gairaigo*　word of foreign origin, loanword　69, 67
外出　　　　*gaishutsu*　go out　　　　　　　　　　　　53
以外　　　　*igai*　besides, except (for)　　　　　　　　46

外　外　外

外 外 外

84	一 イ 冂 (1a) 2a 2r	**NAI, [DAI], uchi** – inside

国内　　　　*kokunai*　domestic, internal　　　　　　　　40
体内　　　　*tainai*　inside the body　　　　　　　　　　61
内外　　　　*naigai*　inner and outer; domestic and foreign　83
年内に　　　*nennai ni*　before the year is out　　　　　　45
一年以内に　*ichinen inai ni*　within a year　　　　　2, 45, 46

内　内　内

内 内 内

85 (1a) 2n 2m	一 ク ト	**SHI** – death; **shi(nu)** – die			
		死 体	*shitai*	dead body, corpse	61
		死 人	*shinin*	dead person, the dead	1
		死 後	*shigo*	after death	48
		水 死	*suishi*	drowning	21
		死 語	*shigo*	dead language	67

86 2d 5b 3d	阝 立 口	**BU** – part, section; copy of a publication			
		一 部	*ichibu*	a part	2
		部 分	*bubun*	a part	38
		大 部 分	*daibubun*	greater part, most	26, 38
		本 部	*honbu*	headquarters	25
		北 部	*hokubu*	the north (of a country)	73

87	亻 立 口 2a 5b 3d	**BAI** – double, times, -fold			
		一 倍	*ichibai*	as much again	2
		二 倍	*nibai*	double, twice as much	3
		三 倍	*sanbai*	3 times as much, threefold	4
		三 倍 以 上	*sanbai ijō*	at least 3 times as much	4, 46, 32
		倍 に す る	*bai ni suru*	double	

倍　倍　倍

倍 倍 倍

88	一 十 丿 1a 2k 1c	**HAN, naka(ba)** – half			
		半 分	*hanbun*	half	38
		半 年	*hantoshi*	half a year, 6 months	45
		三 時 半	*sanjihan*	3:30	4, 42
		前 半	*zenhan, zenpan*	first half	47
		大 半	*taihan*	greater part, majority	26

半　半　半

半 半 半

89	イ 王 2a 4f	**ZEN, matta(ku)** – all, whole, entirely

全部	zenbu	all	86
全国	zenkoku	the whole country	40
全体	zentai	the whole, (in) all	61
全身	zenshin	the entire body	59
万全	banzen	perfect, absolutely sure	16

90	口 刂 3s 3d	**KAI, [E]** – times, repetitions; **mawa(su)** – send around, rotate; **mawa(ru)** – go around, revolve

十回	jikkai	10 times	12
今/前回	kon/zenkai	this/last time	51, 47
言い回し	iimawashi	expression, turn of phrase	66
上回る	uwamawaru	be more than, exceed	32

91	冂 土 口 2r 3b 3d	**SHŪ, mawa(ri)** – lap, circumference; surroundings

一 周　　isshū　　　　1 lap, 1 revolution　　　　　　2
半 周　　hanshū　　　　semicircle, halfway around　　88
円 周　　enshū　　　　　circumference of a circle　　13
百 周 年　hyakushūnen　100th anniversary　　　　14, 45

周　周　周

周　周　周

92	辶 土 口 2q 3b 3d	**SHŪ** – week

二 週 間　nishūkan　　2 weeks　　　　　3, 43
先 週　　senshū　　　last week　　　　50
今 週　　konshū　　　this week　　　　51
来 週　　raishū　　　next week　　　　69
週 日　　shūjitsu　　weekday　　　　　5

週　週　週

週　週　週

93	火 艹 一 4d 3k 1a2	**MU, BU, na(i)** – not be; (prefix) un-, without, -less			
		無名	*mumei*	anonymous; unknown	82
		無口	*mukuchi*	taciturn, laconic	54
		無言	*mugon*	silent, mute	66
		無休	*mukyū*	no holidays, always open (shop)	60
		無事	*buji*	safe and sound	80

94	一 丨 ノ 1a 1b 1c	**FU, BU** – (prefix) not, un-			
		不足	*fusoku*	insufficiency, shortage	58
		不十分	*fujūbun*	not enough, inadequate	12, 38
		行方不明	*yukue fumei*	whereabouts unknown, missing	68, 70, 18
		不当	*futō*	improper, unjust	77
		不死身	*fujimi*	invulnerable	85, 59

95	一 ト |	***CHŌ*** – long; chief, head; ***naga(i)*** – long			
	1a3 2m 1b	部 長	*buchō*	department head, director	86
		身 長	*shinchō*	person's height	59
		長 時 間	*chōjikan*	long time, many hours	42, 43
		長 年	*naganen*	many/long years	45
		長 い 間	*nagai aida*	for a long time	43

96	一 ゛ ノ	***HATSU, HOTSU*** – emit; start from; depart			
	1a3 2o 1c2	発 明	*hatsumei*	invention	18
		発 見	*hakken*	discovery	63
		発 行	*hakkō*	publish, issue	68
		出 発	*shuppatsu*	departure, start out	53
		発 足	*hossoku*	start, inauguration	58

97	心 4k	**SHIN, kokoro** – heart, mind; core		
		中心	*chūshin*	center, midpoint	28
		心身	*shinshin*	body and mind/spirit	59
		本心	*honshin*	one's right mind; real intention	25
		内心	*naishin*	one's inmost heart, true intent	84
		一心に	*isshin ni*	with singlehearted devotion, fervently	2

心 心 心

心 心 心

98	心土一 4k 3b 1a	**SEI** – sex; nature (of); **SHŌ** – temperament		
		中性	*chūsei*	neuter gender	28
		性行	*seikō*	character and conduct	68
		発がん性	*hatsugansei*	carcinogenic, cancer-causing	96
		性分	*seibun*	nature, temperament	38
		本性	*honshō, honsei*	true nature/character	25

性 性 性

性 性 性

99	田 心 5f 4k	**SHI, omo(u)** – think, believe	

思い出　　omoide　　　memories　　53
思い出す　omoidasu　　remember　　53
思い切って　omoikitte　resolutely, daringly　39
思いやり　omoiyari　　compassion, considerateness
思い上がった　omoiagatta　conceited, cocky　32

思　思　思

思 思 思

100	力 2g	**RYOKU, RIKI, chikara** – force, power	

体力　　tairyoku　　physical strength　　61
水力　　suiryoku　　water/hydraulic power　21
風力　　fūryoku　　force of the wind　　29
全力　　zenryoku　　all one's power, utmost efforts　89
無力　　muryoku　　powerless, helpless　93

力 力 力 力 力 力

力 力 力
力 力 力

101	田 力 5f 2g	**DAN, NAN, otoko** – man, human male					
		男性	dansei	man; masculine gender			98
		長男	chōnan	eldest son			95
		男の人	otoko no hito	man			1
		山男	yamaotoko	mountain dweller; mountaineer			34
		大男	ōotoko	giant, tall man			26

102	女 3e	**JO, NYO, [NYŌ], onna** – woman; **me** – feminine					
		女性	josei	woman; feminine gender			98
		長女	chōjo	eldest daughter			95
		男女	danjo	men and women			101
		女中	jochū	maid			28
		女の人	onna no hito	woman			1

103	子 2c	**SHI, SU, ko** – child		

子

男子	*danshi*	boy, man	101
男の子	*otoko no ko*	boy	101
女子	*joshi*	girl, woman	102
女の子	*onna no ko*	girl	102
分子	*bunshi*	molecule; numerator of a fraction	38

104	女 子 3e 2c	**KŌ, kono(mu), su(ku)** – like		

好

好物	*kōbutsu*	favorite food	79
好人物	*kōjinbutsu*	good-natured person	1, 79
物好き	*monozuki*	idle curiosity	79
好き好き	*sukizuki*	matter of individual preference	
大好き	*daisuki*	like very much	26

105	宀 女 3m 3e

AN – peace, peacefulness; *yasu(i)* – cheap

安心	*anshin*	feel relieved/reassured	97
安全	*anzen*	safety	89
不安	*fuan*	unease, anxiety, fear	94
目安	*meyasu*	standard, yardstick	55
安物	*yasumono*	cheap goods	79

106	宀 木 女 3m 4a 3e

AN – plan, proposal

案内	*annai*	guidance, information	84
案外	*angai*	contrary to expectations	83
名案	*meian*	good idea	82
思案	*shian*	consideration, reflection	99
案出	*anshutsu*	contrive, devise	53

107	冂 十 一 2r 2k 1a	**YŌ** – business; usage; **mochi(iru)** – use		
用		用 事　　　yōji　　　business affair; errand		80
		用 水　　　yōsui　　　city/tap water		21
		用 語　　　yōgo　　　(technical) term, vocabulary		67
		無 用　　　muyō　　　useless; unnecessary		93
		男 子 用　　danshiyō　　for men, men's		101, 103

108	雨 日 丨 8d 4c 1b	**DEN** – electricity		
電		電 力　　denryoku　　electrical power/energy		100
		電 子　　denshi　　electron		103
		発 電　　hatsuden　　generation of electricity		96
		外 電　　gaiden　　telegram from abroad		83

109	⺍ 冖 子 3n 2i 2c	**GAKU** – science, study; **mana(bu)** – learn		

大学 　　daigaku 　university, college 　26
学部 　　gakubu 　academic department; faculty 　86
入学 　　nyūgaku 　entry/admission into a school 　52
学生 　　gakusei 　student 　44
語学 　　gogaku 　linguistics 　67

学 学 学

学

学 学 学

110	宀 子 3m 2c	**JI** – character, letter; **aza** – village section		

国字 　　kokuji 　national/Japanese script 　40
当て字 　ateji 　kanji used phonetically/for meaning 　77
ローマ字 rōmaji 　roman letters
字体 　　jitai 　form of a character, type font 　61
十字 　　jūji 　a cross 　12

字 字 字

字 字 字

111	亠 丿 丶 2j 1c 1d	**BUN, MON** – literature, text, sentence; *fumi* – letter, note

文字　　　　*moji, monji*　letter, character　　　　　　110
文学　　　　*bungaku*　literature　　　　　　　　　　109
本文　　　　*honbun, honmon*　text, wording　　　　　25
文語　　　　*bungo*　the written language　　　　　　67
文明　　　　*bunmei*　civilization　　　　　　　　　　18

文　文　文

文　文　文

112	一 丿 丶 1a2 1c 1d2	**BO, haha** – mother

母子　　　　*boshi*　mother and child　　　　　　　　103
生母　　　　*seibo*　one's biological mother　　　　　44
母国語　　　*bokokugo*　one's mother tongue　　　40, 67
母方　　　　*hahakata*　on the mother's side, maternal　70
お母さん　　*okāsan*　mother

母　母　母　母　母

母　母　母

113	` ノ ` 2o 1c 1d	**FU, chichi** – father

FU, chichi – father

父母	fubo	father and mother	112
父子	fushi	father and child/son	103
父方	chichikata	on the father's side, paternal	70
父上	chichiue	father	32
お父さん	otōsan	father	

114	亠 ` ノ 2j 2o 1c	**KŌ** – intersection; coming and going; *ma(jiru/zaru)* – (intr.) mix; *maji(eru)*, *ma(zeru)* – (tr.) mix; *maji(waru), ka(u)* – associate (with); *ka(wasu)* – exchange (greetings)

国交	kokkō	diplomatic relations	40
外交	gaikō	foreign policy, diplomacy	83
性交	seikō	sexual intercourse	98

115	木 宀 丷 4a 2j 2o	**KŌ** – school; (printing) proof		
		学校	gakkō	school	109
		小学校	shōgakkō	elementary school	27, 109
		中学校	chūgakkō	junior high school	28, 109
		母校	bokō	alma mater	112
		校長	kōchō	principal, headmaster	95

校　校　校

校　校　校

116	一 ノ 1a3 1c3	**MAI** – every, each		
		毎年	mainen, maitoshi	every year, yearly, annual	45
		毎月	maigetsu, maitsuki	every month, monthly	17
		毎週	maishū	every week, weekly	92
		毎日	mainichi	every day, daily	5
		毎時	maiji	every hour, hourly, per hour	42

毎　毎　毎　毎　毎

毎　毎　毎

117	氵 一 ノ 3a 1a3 1c3	***KAI, umi*** – sea, ocean			
		大 海	*taikai*	an ocean	26
		海 上	*kaijō*	ocean, seagoing, marine	32
		海 外	*kaigai*	overseas, abroad	83
		内 海	*uchiumi, naikai*	inland sea	84
		日 本 海	*Nihonkai*	Sea of Japan	5, 25

海　海　海　海　海　海

海　海　海

118	土 丨 ノ 3b 1b2 1c	***CHI, JI*** – earth, land			
		土 地	*tochi*	land, soil	24
		地 下	*chika*	underground, subterranean	31
		地 方	*chihō*	region, area	70
		地 名	*chimei*	place name	82
		生 地	*kiji*	material, cloth	44

地　地　地

地　地　地

119	氵 丨 ノ 3a 1b2 1c	**CHI, ike** – pond

用水池　yōsuichi　water reservoir　107, 21
電池　denchi　battery　108
池田　Ikeda　(surname)　35

池

池　池　池

池 池 池

120	イ 丨 ノ 2a 1b2 1c	**TA** – other, another

他人　tanin　another person; stranger　1
他国　takoku　another/foreign country　40
他方　tahō　the other side/party/direction　70
自他　jita　oneself and others　62
その他　sonota　and so forth

他

他　他　他

他 他 他

121	立 5b	*RITSU, [RYŪ], ta(tsu)* – stand (up); *ta(teru)* – set up, raise

国立	*kokuritsu*	national, state-supported	40
自立	*jiritsu*	independent, self-supporting	62
中立	*chūritsu*	neutral, neutrality	28
目立つ	*medatsu*	be conspicuous, stick out	55
立ち上がる	*tachiagaru*	stand up	32

122	亻立 2a 5b	*I, kurai* – rank, position

地位	*chii*	position, rank	118
学位	*gakui*	academic degree	109
上位	*jōi*	higher rank	32
本位	*hon'i*	monetary standard; basis, principle	25
位取り	*kuraidori*	position (before/after decimal point)	65

123 - 124

123	氵 土 丿
	3a 3b 1c

HŌ, HA', HO' – law

国法	kokuhō	laws of the country	40
立法	rippō	enactment of legislation	121
法案	hōan	bill, legislative proposal	106
文法	bunpō	grammar	111
方法	hōhō	method	70

法　法　法

法　法　法

124	禾 口
	5d 3d

WA, [O] – peace, harmony; **yawa(rageru/ragu), nago(mu)** – soften, calm down; **nago(yaka)** – mild, gentle, congenial

和文	wabun	Japanese script	111
和風	wafū	Japanese style	29
不和	fuwa	disharmony, discord, enmity	94
大和	Yamato	(old) Japan	26

和　和　和

和　和　和

125	禾 ノ 丶 5d 1c 1d	**SHI, watakushi** – I; private

私事	shiji	personal affairs	80
私物	shibutsu	private property	79
私用	shiyō	private use	107
私立	shiritsu	private, privately supported	121
私自身	watakushi jishin	personally, as for me	62, 59

126	丶 ノ 丶 2o 1c 1d	**KŌ, ōyake** – public, official

公安	kōan	public peace/security	105
公法	kōhō	public law	123
公立	kōritsu	public	121
公海	kōkai	international waters	117
公言	kōgen	public declaration, avowal	66

127	木 4a2	**RIN, hayashi** – woods, forest

山林	*sanrin*	mountains and forests; mountain forest	34
(山)林学	*(san)ringaku*	forestry	34, 109
林立	*rinritsu*	stand close together in large numbers	121
小林	*Kobayashi*	(surname)	27

128	木 4a3	**SHIN, mori** – woods, forest

| 森林 | *shinrin* | woods, forest | 127 |
| 大森 | *Ōmori* | (area of Tokyo) | 26 |

129	⺮ 6f	**CHIKU, take** – bamboo

竹 林	*chikurin, takebayashi*	bamboo grove/thicket	127
竹 刀	*shinai*	bamboo sword (for Kendo)	37
さお竹	*saodake*	bamboo pole	
竹のつえ	*take no tsue*	bamboo cane	
竹やぶ	*takeyabu*	bamboo thicket	

竹　竹　竹

竹　竹　竹

130	⺮ 十 一 6f　2k　1a4	**HITSU, fude** – writing brush

万 年 筆	*mannenhitsu*	fountain pen	16, 45
自 筆	*jihitsu*	one's own handwriting; autograph	62
筆 名	*hitsumei*	pen name, pseudonym	82
文 筆	*bunpitsu*	literary work, writing	111
筆 先	*fudesaki*	tip of the writing brush	50

筆　筆　筆

筆　筆　筆

131	日 土 一	**SHO, ka(ku)** – write		
	4c 3b 1a3	書物 *shomotsu* book		79
		文書 *bunsho* (in) writing, document		111
		書名 *shomei* book title		82
		前書き *maegaki* foreword, preface		47
		書き取り *kakitori* dictation		65

132	立 日 心	**I** – will, heart, mind, thought; meaning, sense		
	5b 4c 4k	意見 *iken* opinion		63
		用意 *yōi* preparations, readiness		107
		好意 *kōi* goodwill, good wishes, kindness		104
		意外 *igai* unexpected, surprising		83
		不意 *fui* sudden, unexpected		94

133	車 7c	**SHA, kuruma** – vehicle; wheel

電 車	*densha*	electric train	108
人 力 車	*jinrikisha*	rickshaw	1, 100
発 車	*hassha*	departure	96
下 車	*gesha*	get off (a train)	31
水 車	*suisha*	waterwheel	21

134	一 ノ 、 1a3 1c2 1d	**KI, KE** – spirit, soul, mood

人 気	*ninki*	popularity	1
気 分	*kibun*	feeling, mood	38
本 気	*honki*	seriousness, (in) earnest	25
気 体	*kitai*	a gas	61
電 気	*denki*	electricity	108

| 135 | 氵 一 丿
 3a 1a3 1c | *KI* – steam
 汽車　　　*kisha*　　　train drawn by steam locomotive　　　133 |

| 136 | 厂 日 ⺮
 2p 4c 3n | *GEN* – original, fundamental; *hara* – plain, field; wilderness
 原案　　　*gen'an*　　　the original plan/proposal　　　106
 原書　　　*gensho*　　　(in) the original (text)　　　131
 原文　　　*genbun*　　　the text, the original　　　111
 原生林　　　*genseirin*　　　primeval/virgin forest　　　44, 127
 原子　　　*genshi*　　　atom　　　103 |

137	一 ` 1a2 2o	**_GEN_** – yuan, yüan (Chinese monetary unit); **_GAN, moto_** – origin, foundation

元日 　*ganjitsu*　New Year's Day　5
元金 　*gankin*　principal (vs. interest)　23
元気 　*genki*　healthy, peppy　134
地元 　*jimoto*　local　118

元 元 元

元 元 元

138	` ` 一 3n 2o 1a	**_KŌ, hikari_** – light; **_hika(ru)_** – shine

日光 　*nikkō*　sunlight, sunshine　5
月光 　*gekkō*　moonlight　17
光年 　*kōnen*　light-year　45
発光 　*hakkō*　luminosity, emit light　96
電光 　*denkō*　electric light, lightning　108

光 光 光

光 光 光

139	一 丨 1a2 1b	**KŌ, KU** – artisan; manufacturing, construction

工事 (中)	*kōji(chū)*	(under) construction	80, 28
大 工	*daiku*	carpenter	26
女 工	*jokō*	woman factory-worker	102
工 学	*kōgaku*	engineering	109
人 工	*jinkō*	man-made, artificial	1

工　工　工

工　工　工

140	宀 ソ 一 3m 2o 1a2	**KŪ, sora** – sky; **a(keru/ku)** – make/be unoccupied; **kara** – empty

空 気	*kūki*	air	134
(時 間 と) 空 間	*(jikan to) kūkan*	(time and) space	42, 43
空 車	*kūsha*	empty car, For Hire (taxi)	133
空 手	*karate*	empty-handed; karate	57
大 空	*ōzora*	sky, firmament	26

空　空　空

空　空　空

141	一 亻
	1a2 2a

TEN, ame, [ama] – heaven

天 気	tenki	weather	134
天 文 学	tenmongaku	astronomy	111, 109
天 国	tengoku	paradise	40
天 性	tensei	nature, natural constitution	98
天 の 川	amanogawa	Milky Way	33

142	一 日 土
	(1a) 4c 3b

RI – (old unit of length, about 2.9 km); **sato** – village; one's parents' home

千 里	senri	1,000 ri; a great distance	15
海 里	kairi	nautical mile	117
里 子	satogo	foster child	103
里 心	satogokoro	homesickness	97

143 王 日 土 4f 4c 3b	**RI** – reason, logic, principle	
	地 理 (学) *chiri(gaku)* geography	118, 109
	心 理 学 *shinrigaku* psychology	97, 109
	理 学 部 *rigakubu* department of science	109, 86
	無 理 *muri* unreasonable; impossible; (by) force	93
	理 事 *riji* director	80

144 ⺌ ノ 3n 1c	**SHŌ, suko(shi)** – a little; **suku(nai)** – little, few, slight	
	少 年 *shōnen* boy	45
	少 年 法 *shōnenhō* the Juvenile Law	45, 123
	少 女 *shōjo* girl	102
	少 々 *shōshō* a little	
	少 し ず つ *sukoshizutsu* little by little, a little at a time	

| 145 | 目 ⸌⸍ ノ
5c 3n 1c | **SEI, kaeri(miru)** – reflect upon, give heed to; **SHŌ** – (government) ministry;
habu(ku) – omit; cut down on |

自省	jisei	reflection, introspection	62
内省	naisei	introspection	84
人事不省	jinjifusei	unconsciousness, fainting	1, 80, 94
文部省	Monbushō	Ministry of Education	111, 86

| 146 | 木 目
4a 5c | **SŌ** – aspect, phase; **SHŌ** – (government) minister; **ai-** – together, fellow, each
other |

相当	sōtō	suitable, appropriate	77
文相	bunshō	minister of education	111
外相	gaishō	foreign minister	83
相手	aite	the other party, partner, opponent	57

147	心 目 木 4k 5c 4a	**SŌ, [SO]** – idea, thought		

思 想　shisō　idea, thought　99
回 想　kaisō　retrospection, reminiscence　90
理 想　risō　an ideal　143
空 想　kūsō　fantasy, daydream　140
めい想　meisō　meditation

想　想　想

想　想　想

148	⼆ 目 一 2o 5c 1a	**SHU, kubi** – neck, head		

首 相　shushō　prime minister　146
元 首　genshu　sovereign, ruler　137
首 位　shui　leading position, top spot　122
部 首　bushu　radical of a kanji　86
手 首　tekubi　wrist　57

首　首　首

首　首　首

149	辶 目 丷
	2q 5c 2o

DŌ, [TŌ], michi – street, way, path

国道	kokudō	national highway	40
水道	suidō	water conduits, running water	21
北海道	Hokkaidō	(northernmost of the 4 main islands	73, 117
書道	shodō	calligraphy ⌊of Japan)	131
回り道	mawarimichi	a detour	

道 道 道 道 道

道 道 道

150	辶 冂 十
	2q 2r 2k

TSŪ, [TSU], tō(ru) – go through, pass; **tō(su)** – let through; **kayo(u)** – commute

交通	kōtsū	traffic, transportation	114
文通	buntsū	correspondence, exchange of letters	111
通学	tsūgaku	attend school	109
見通し	mitōshi	prospects, outlook	63

通 通 通

通 通 通

151	足 攵 口	**RO, -ji** – street, way
	7d 4i 3d	

道 路	dōro	street, road	149
十 字 路	jūjiro	intersection, crossroads	12, 110
水 路	suiro	waterway, aqueduct	21
海 路	kairo	sea route	117
通 路	tsūro	passageway, walkway, aisle	150

152	戸	**KO, to** – door
	4m	

戸 外 で	kogai de	outdoors, in the open air	83
下 戸	geko	nondrinker, teetotaler	31
戸 口	toguchi	doorway	54
木 戸	kido	gate, entrance; castle gate	22
雨 戸	amado	storm door, shutter	30

153	戸 厂 一	**SHO, tokoro** – place			
	4m 2p 1a	案内所	*annaijo*	inquiry office, information desk	106, 84
		名所	*meisho*	noted place, sights (to see)	82
		所長	*shochō*	director, head, manager	95
		長所	*chōsho*	strong point, merit, advantage	95
		発電所	*hatsudensho*	power plant	96, 108

所　所　所

所　所　所

154	土 日 一	**JŌ, ba** – place			
	3b 4c 1a2	工場	*kōjō, kōba*	factory, plant	139
		出場	*shutsujō*	stage appearance; participation	53
		場所	*basho*	place, location	153
		立ち場	*tachiba*	standpoint, point of view	121
		相場	*sōba*	market price	146

場　場　場

場　場　場

155	主 丶 4f 1d	**SHU, [SU], *nushi*** – lord, master; main; ***omo*** – main, principal

主人	*shujin*	husband, head of household	1
主人公	*shujinkō*	hero, main character	1, 126
自主	*jishu*	independence, autonomy	62
主語	*shugo*	subject (in grammar)	67
地主	*jinushi*	landowner, landlord	118

主　主　主

主　主　主

156	亻主 丶 2a 4f 1d	**JŪ, *su(mu/mau)*** – live, dwell, reside

住所	*jūsho*	an address	153
住人	*jūnin*	inhabitant, resident	1
安住	*anjū*	peaceful living	105
住まい	*sumai*	residence, where one lives, address	
住み心地	*sumigokochi*	comfortableness, livability	97, 118

住　住　住

住　住　住

157	イ 言 2a 7a	**SHIN** – faith, trust, belief			
		信用	shin'yō	trust	107
		不信	fushin	bad faith, insincerity; distrust	94
		自信	jishin	(self-)confidence	62
		所信	shoshin	one's conviction, opinion	153
		通信	tsūshin	communication, correspondence, dispatch	150

158	イ 一 ノ 2a 1a2 1c	**KAI** – meeting; association; **E, a(u)** – meet			
		国会	kokkai	parliament, diet, congress	40
		大会	taikai	mass meeting; sports meet, tournament	26
		学会	gakkai	learned/academic society	109
		会見	kaiken	interview, news conference	63
		出会う	deau	happen to meet, run into	53

159	イ 口 一 2a 3d 1a	**GŌ, GA', [KA'], a(u)** – fit; **a(waseru/wasu)** – put together		
		合意	*gōi*	mutual consent, agreement	132
		場合	*baai, bawai*	(in this) case	154
		(お)見合い	*(o)miai*	marriage interview	63
		見合わせる	*miawaseru*	look at each other; postpone	63
		間に合う	*ma ni au*	be in time (for); will do, suffice	43

合　合　合

合　合　合

160	⺮ 口 イ 6f 3d 2a	**TŌ, kota(e)** – an answer; **kota(eru)** – answer		
		回答	*kaitō*	an answer, reply	90
		口答	*kōtō*	oral answer	54
		筆答	*hittō*	written answer	130
		名答	*meitō*	correct answer	82
		答案	*tōan*	examination paper	106

答　答　答

答　答　答

161	門 8e	**MON, kado** – gate		
		入門(書)	*nyūmon(sho)*	introduction, primer	52, 131
		部門	*bumon*	group, category, branch	86
		名門	*meimon*	distinguished/illustrious family	82
		門下生	*monkasei*	(someone's) pupil	31, 44
		門口	*kadoguchi*	front door, entrance	54

162	問 8e 3d	**MON, to(i), [ton]** – question, problem; **to(u)** – matter, care about		
		問答	*mondō*	questions and answers, dialogue	160
		学問	*gakumon*	learning, science	109
		問い合わせる	*toiawaseru*	inquire, ask	159
		問いただす	*toitadasu*	inquire, question	

163	口 貝 3d 7b	**IN** – member		
		会 員　　*kaiin*　　member (of a society)		158
		海 員　　*kaiin*　　seaman, sailor		117
		工 員　　*kōin*　　factory worker		139
		人 員　　*jin'in*　　staff, personnel		1
		全 員　　*zen'in*　　all members, entire staff		89

164	日 土 ノ 4c 3b 1c	**SHA, mono** – person		
		学 者　　*gakusha*　　scholar		109
		日 本 学 者　*Nihongakusha*　Japanologist		5, 25, 109
		筆 者　　*hissha*　　writer, author		130
		信 者　　*shinja*　　believer, the faithful		157
		後 者　　*kōsha*　　the latter		48

165	宀 一 ノ 3m 1a 1c4	**KA, KE, ie, ya** – house; family			
		家事	kaji	family affairs; household chores	80
		家内	kanai	(one's own) wife	84
		家来	kerai	retainer, vassal	69
		国家	kokka	state, nation	40
		家主	yanushi	landlord, house owner	155

166	宀 土 一 3m 3b 1a	**SHITSU** – a room; **muro** – greenhouse; cellar			
		和室	washitsu	Japanese-style room	124
		私室	shishitsu	private room	125
		室内	shitsunai	in a room, indoor	84
		分室	bunshitsu	isolated room; annex	38
		室長	shitsuchō	senior roommate; section chief	95

167	尸 土 一 3r 3b 1a	***OKU, ya*** – roof, house; shop, dealer		

屋

家屋　　*kaoku*　　house, building　　165
屋上　　*okujō*　　roof, rooftop　　32
部屋　　*heya*　　a room　　86
小屋　　*koya*　　cottage, hut, shack　　27
八百屋　*yaoya*　vegetable shop, greengrocer　10, 14

屋 屋 屋

屋 屋 屋

168	广 口 卜 3q 3d 2m	***TEN, mise*** – shop, store		

店

書店　　*shoten*　　bookstore　　131
本店　　*honten*　　head office, main shop　　25
店員　　*ten'in*　　store employee, clerk　　163
店先　　*misesaki*　storefront　　50
出店　　*demise*　　branch store　　53

店 店 店

店 店 店

169	ト 火 口 2m 4d 3d	**TEN** – point			
		出発点	*shuppatsuten*	starting point	53, 96
		原点	*genten*	starting point; origin (of coordinates)	136
		合点	*gaten, gatten*	understanding; consent	159
		点字	*tenji*	Braille	110
		点火	*tenka*	ignite	20

170	尸 口 一 3r 3d 1a	**KYOKU** – bureau, office			
		当局	*tōkyoku*	the authorities, responsible officials	77
		局長	*kyokuchō*	director of a bureau; postmaster	95
		局員	*kyokuin*	staff member of a bureau	163
		局外者	*kyokugaisha*	outsider, onlooker	83, 164
		時局	*jikyoku*	the situation	42

171	尸 口 十 3r 3d 2k	**KYO, i(ru)** – be (present), exist		
		住居	jūkyo	dwelling, residence	156
		居住地	kyojūchi	place of residence	156, 118
		居間	ima	living room	43
		長居	nagai	stay (too) long	95
		居合わせる	iawaseru	(happen to) be present	159

居　居　居

居　居　居

172	十 口 2k 3d	**KO, furu(i)** – old; **furu(su)** – wear out		
		古風	kofū	old customs; antiquated	29
		古語	kogo	archaic word; old adage	67
		古文	kobun	classical literature, ancient classics	111
		古今東西	kokon-tōzai	all ages and countries	51, 71, 72
		古本	furuhon	secondhand/used book	25

古　古　古

古　古　古

173	攵 口 十 4i 3d 2k	**KO** – deceased; **yue** – reason, cause; circumstances

故人　　　*kojin*　　　the deceased　　　　　　　　　　1
故事　　　*koji*　　　historical　　　　　　　　　　　80
事故　　　*jiko*　　　accident　　　　　　　　　　　80
故国　　　*kokoku*　　one's homeland, native country　40
故意　　　*koi*　　　intention, purpose　　　　　　　132

174	立 木 厂 5b 4a 2p	**SHIN, atara(shii), ara(ta), nii-** – new

新聞　　　　*shinbun*　　　newspaper　　　　　　　64
古新聞　　　*furushinbun*　old newspapers　　　　172
新年　　　　*shinnen*　　　the New Year　　　　　45
新人　　　　*shinjin*　　　newcomer, new face　　　1
一新　　　　*isshin*　　　renovation, reform　　　2

175	立 目 木 5b 5c 4a	**SHIN** – intimacy; parent; *oya* – parent; *shita(shii)* – intimate, close (friend); *shita(shimu)* – get to know better

親切	shinsetsu	kind, friendly	39
親日	shin-Nichi	pro-Japanese	5
母親	hahaoya	mother	112
親子	oyako	parent and child	103

親　親　親　　　　姑

親　親　親

176	貝 厂 一 7b 2p2 1a2	**SHITSU** – quality, nature; **SHICHI, [CHI]** – hostage; pawn

質問	shitsumon	a question	162
性質	seishitsu	nature, property	98
物質	busshitsu	matter, material, substance	79
本質	honshitsu	essence, substance	25
人質	hitojichi	hostage	1

質　質　質

質　質　質

177	一 尸 丶 1a 3r 1d	**MIN, tami** – people, nation		

国民	kokumin	people, nation, citizen	40
人民	jinmin	the people, citizens	1
(原)住民	(gen)jūmin	(aboriginal) native of a place	136, 156
民間	minkan	private (not public)	43
民意	min'i	will of the people	132

民　民　民

民　民　民

178	宀 丨 ノ 3m 1b 1c2	**TAKU** – house, home, residence		

住宅	jūtaku	house, residence	156
自宅	jitaku	one's own home, private residence	62
私宅	shitaku	one's private residence	125
宅地	takuchi	land for housing, residential site	118
家宅	kataku	house, the premises	165

宅　宅　宅

宅　宅　宅

179	宀 日 亻 3m 4c 2a	**SHUKU, yado** – lodging, inn; **yado(ru)** – take shelter; be pregnant; **yado(su)** – give shelter; conceive (a child)				
宿		下 宿	*geshuku*	room and board; boardinghouse		31
		合 宿	*gasshuku*	lodging together		159
		民 宿	*minshuku*	private house providing tourist lodging		177
		宿 屋	*yadoya*	inn		167

宿	宿	宿							
宿	宿	宿							

180	糸 厂 一 6a 2p 1a	**SHI, kami** – paper			
紙		和 紙	*washi*	Japanese paper	124
		日 本 紙	*nihonshi*	Japanese paper	5, 25
		新 聞 紙	*shinbunshi*	newspaper; newsprint	174, 64
		質 問 用 紙	*shitsumon yōshi*	questionnaire	176, 162, 107
		手 紙	*tegami*	letter	57

紙	紙	紙							
紙	紙	紙							

181	亠 巾 2j 3f	**SHI** – city; **ichi** – market

市長　shichō　mayor　95
市会　shikai　municipal assembly, city council　158
市立　shiritsu　municipal　121
市民　shimin　citizen, townspeople　177
市場　ichiba, shijō　marketplace, market　154

市　市　市

市　市　市

182	田 一 丨 5f 1a 1b	**CHŌ, machi** – town, quarter

町民　chōmin　townsman, townsfolk　177
町人　chōnin　merchant; townsfolk　1
町内　chōnai　neighborhood　84
下町　shitamachi　(low-lying) downtown area　31
室町　Muromachi　(historical period, 1392–1573)　166

町　町　町

町　町　町

183	匚 ノ 、 2t 1c 1d	**KU** – municipal administrative district, ward

地区	*chiku*	district, area, zone		118
区間	*kukan*	section, interval		43
区切る	*kugiru*	partition; punctuate		39
区分	*kubun*	division, partition; classification		38
北区	*Kita-ku*	Kita Ward (Tokyo)		73

区

区	区	区						

区	区	区											

184	一 丨 1a 1b	**CHŌ** – even number; (counter for blocks of houses/blocks of tofu/guns/dishes of prepared food); **TEI** – D, No. 4 (in a series); adult; ⊤ shape

丁目	*chōme*	city block (in addresses)		55
丁年	*teinen*	(age of) majority, adulthood		45
丁字路	*teijiro*	⊤-shaped street intersection		110, 151

丁

丁	丁	丁						

丁	丁	丁											

185	米 田 ノ 6b 5f 1c

BAN – keeping watch; number, order

一番	*ichiban*	the first; number one, most	2
二番目	*nibanme*	the second, No. 2	3, 55
番地	*banchi*	lot/house number	118
局番	*kyokuban*	exchange (part of a phone number)	170
交番	*kōban*	police box	114

186	彳 土 一 3i 3b2 1a2

GAI, [KAI], machi – street

街路	*gairo*	street	151
街道	*kaidō*	street, highway	149
市街	*shigai*	the streets (of a city); town	181
名店街	*meitengai*	arcade of well-known stores	82, 168
地下街	*chikagai*	underground shopping mall	118, 31

187	彳 木 一 3i 4a 1a2	*JUTSU* – art, technique; means; conjury

手術　　　　*shujutsu*　　　(surgical) operation　　　　　　　　　57
手術室　　　*shujutsushitsu*　operating room　　　　　　　　　57, 166
学術　　　　*gakujutsu*　　　science, learning　　　　　　　　　109
(学) 術 (用) 語　*(gaku)jutsu(yō)go*　technical term, terminology 109, 107, 67

術　術　術

術　術　術

188	阝 日 土 2d 4c 3b	*TO, TSU, miyako* – capital (city)

(大) 都 市　　*(dai)toshi*　　(major/large) city　　　　　　　　26, 181
都 会　　　　*tokai*　　　　city　　　　　　　　　　　　　　　158
首 都　　　　*shuto*　　　　capital (city)　　　　　　　　　　148
都 内　　　　*tonai*　　　　in (the city of) Tokyo　　　　　　　84
都 合　　　　*tsugō*　　　　circumstances, reasons　　　　　　159

都　都　都

都　都　都

189	亠 口 ⸌⸍ 2j 3d 3n	**KYŌ, KEI** – the capital

東 京 (都)　　*Tōkyō(-to)*　　(City of) Tokyo　　　　　71, 188
京 都 (市)　　*Kyōto(-shi)*　　(City of) Kyoto　　　　188, 181
上 京　　　　*jōkyō*　　　　go/come to Tokyo　　　　32
北 京　　　　*Pekin*　　　　Peking, Beijing　　　　　73
南 京　　　　*Nankin*　　　　Nanking　　　　　　　74

京　　京　京

京 京 京

190	亠 口 冂 2j 3d2 2r	**KŌ, taka(i)** – high; expensive; **taka** – amount, quantity; **taka(maru)** – rise; **taka(meru)** – raise

高 原　　　　*kōgen*　　　plateau, heights, tableland　　136
高 校　　　　*kōkō*　　　senior high school (cf. No. 569)　115
名 高 い　　　*nadakai*　　renowned, famous　　　　　82

高　　高　高

高 高 高

191	木 十 丶 4a 2k 1d	**SON, mura** – village				

市町村　*shichōson*　cities, towns, and villages　181, 182
村会　*sonkai*　village assembly　158
村長　*sonchō*　village mayor　95
村民　*sonmin*　villager　177
村人　*murabito*　villager　1

192	亻 十 丶 2a 2k 1d	**FU, tsu(ku)** – be attached, belong (to); **tsu(keru)** – attach, apply (cf. No. 1843)				

交付　*kōfu*　deliver, hand over　114
日付け　*hizuke*　date (of a letter)　5
気付く　*kizuku*　(take) notice　134
付き物　*tsukimono*　what (something) entails, adjunct　79

193	阝 口 厂 2d 3d 2p	**GUN** – county, district

郡部　　　*gunbu*　　　rural district　　　　　　　　　　　86
新田郡　　*Nitta-gun*　　Nitta District (in Gunma Prefecture)　　174, 35

郡　郡　郡

郡　郡　郡

194	⺍ 目 丨 3n 5c 1b	**KEN** – prefecture, province

郡県　　　*gunken*　　　districts/counties and prefectures　　193
県立　　　*kenritsu*　　prefectural, provincial　　　　　　121
県道　　　*kendō*　　　prefectural highway　　　　　　　149
県会　　　*kenkai*　　　prefectural assembly　　　　　　158
山口県　　*Yamaguchi-ken*　Yamaguchi Prefecture　　　　34, 54

県　県　県

県　県　県

195	リ 丨 丶 2f 1b2 1d2	**SHŪ** – state, province; *su* – sandbank, shoals		
		本州	*Honshū*	(largest of the 4 main islands of Japan) 25
		カリフォルニア州	*Kariforunia-shū*	(State of) California
		五大州	*godaishū*	Asia, Africa, Europe, America, and Australia 7, 26
		中州	*nakasu*	sandbank in a river 28

州

州　州　州

州 州 州

196	艹 丷 一 3k 2o 1a	**KYŌ, tomo** – together, both, all		
		共学	*kyōgaku*	coeducation 109
		共通	*kyōtsū*	(in) common (with) 150
		公共	*kōkyō*	the public, community 126
		共和国	*kyōwakoku*	republic 124, 40

共

共　共　共

共 共 共

197	イ ⺾ ⺌ 2a 3k 2o	**KYŌ, [KU], _tomo_** – retinue, attendant; serve; **_sona(eru)_** – offer

供

供 出	_kyōshutsu_	delivery	53
自 供	_jikyō_	confession, admission	62
供 物	_kumotsu_	votive offering	79
子 供	_kodomo_	child	103
(お) 供	_(o)tomo_	accompany (someone)	

供 供 供

供供供

198	⺆ ⼝ 一 2r 3d 1a	**DŌ, _ona(ji)_** – same

同

同 時 に	_dōji ni_	at the same time, simultaneously	42
共 同	_kyōdō_	joint, communal, cooperative	196
合 同	_gōdō_	combination, merger, joint	159
同 意	_dōi_	agreement, consent	132
同 居	_dōkyo_	live in the same house	171

同 同 同

同同同

199	⺊ ⎕ ノ
	3d 2r 1c

KŌ, mu(kau) – face (toward); proceed (to); **mu(ku/keru)** – (intr./tr.) turn; **mu(kō)** – opposite side

方向	hōkō	direction	70
向上	kōjō	elevation, betterment	32
意向	ikō	intention, inclination	132
外人向け	gaijinmuke	for foreigners	83, 1

200	一 ⼳ ⎕
	1a 3o 2r

RYŌ – both; (obsolete Japanese coin)

両親	ryōshin	parents	175
両方	ryōhō	both	70
両手	ryōte	both hands	57
両立	ryōritsu	coexist, be compatible (with)	121
車両	sharyō	car, vehicle	133

201	氵 艹 山 3a 3k 3o	**MAN, mi(chiru)** – become full; **mi(tasu)** – fill; fulfill		
		満足	*manzoku*	satisfaction	58
		不満	*fuman*	dissatisfaction, discontent	94
		満員	*man'in*	full to capacity	163
		満点	*manten*	perfect score	169
		円満	*enman*	harmonious, peaceful, perfect	13

満

満	満	満							

満	満	満									

202	十 一 ノ 2k 1a 1c	**HEI, BYŌ, tai(ra), hira** – flat, level		
		平行	*heikō*	parallel	68
		平和	*heiwa*	peace	124
		不平	*fuhei*	discontent, complaint	94
		平家	*Heike*	(historical clan name)	165
			hiraya	1-story house	

平

平	平	平							

平	平	平									

203	宀 亻 一 3m 2a 1a3	***JITSU*** – truth, actuality; ***mi*** – fruit, nut; ***mino(ru)*** – bear fruit		
		事 実	*jijitsu*	fact	80
		口 実	*kōjitsu*	pretext, excuse	54
		実 行	*jikkō*	put into practice, carry out, realize	68
		実 力	*jitsuryoku*	actual ability, competence	100
		実 用	*jitsuyō*	practical use	107

204	⺈ 一 丨 2n 1a2 1b2	***SHOKU, SHIKI, iro*** – color; erotic passion		
		原 色	*genshoku*	primary color	136
		好 色	*kōshoku*	sensuality, lust, eroticism	104
		色 紙	*shikishi*	(type of calligraphy paper)	180
			irogami	colored paper	
		金 色	*kin'iro, kinshoku, konjiki* gold color		23

205	日 ノ 4c 1c	***HAKU, BYAKU, shiro(i), shiro, [shira]* – white**		
		白 紙	*hakushi*	white/blank paper	180
		白 書	*hakusho*	a white paper (on), report	131
		白 人	*hakujin*	a white, Caucasian	1
		自 白	*jihaku*	confession, admission	62
		空 白	*kūhaku*	a blank; vacuum	140

白 白 白

白 白 白

206	火 日 土 4d 4c 3b	***KOKU, kuro(i), kuro* – black**		
		黒 人	*kokujin*	a black, Negro	1
		黒 白	*kuroshiro, kokubyaku* black and/or white; right and wrong	205
		黒 字	*kuroji*	(in the) black, black figures	120
		黒 子	*kuroko*	black-clad Kabuki stagehand	103

黒 黒 黒

黒 黒 黒

207	土 丨 ノ 3b 1b2 1c	***SEKI, [SHAKU], aka(i), aka*** – red; ***aka(ramu)*** – become red, blush; ***aka(rameru)*** – make red, blush

赤十字	*Sekijūji*	Red Cross	12, 110
赤道	*sekidō*	equator	149
赤字	*akaji*	deficit, red figures, (in the) red	110
赤ちゃん	*akachan*	baby	

208	月 土 一 4b 3b 1a	***SEI, [SHŌ], ao(i), ao*** – blue, green; unripe

青年	*seinen*	young man/people	45
青少年	*seishōnen*	young people, youth	144, 45
青空	*aozora*	blue sky	140
青空市場	*aozora ichiba*	open-air market	140, 181, 154
青物	*aomono*	green vegetables	79

209	心 月 土 4k 4b 3b

JŌ, [SEI], nasa(ke) – emotion, sympathy; circumstances

人 情	ninjō	human feelings, humanity	1
同 情	dōjō	sympathy	198
無 情	mujō	heartlessness, callousness	93
事 情	jijō	circumstances, situation	80
実 情	jitsujō	actual situation, the facts	203

210	日 一 ノ 4c 1a 1c2

TEKI – (attributive suffix); **mato** – target

目 的	mokuteki	purpose, aim, goal	55
一 時 的	ichijiteki	temporary	2, 42
民 主 的	minshuteki	democratic	177, 155
理 想 的	risōteki	ideal	143, 147
自 発 的	jihatsuteki	voluntary, spontaneous	62, 96

211	糸 一 ｜ 6a 1a 1b	**YAKU** – approximately; promise

	公約	*kōyaku*	public commitment	126
	口約	*kōyaku*	verbal promise	54
	先約 (が ある)	*sen'yaku (ga aru)*	(have a) previous engagement	50
	約半分	*yaku hanbun*	approximately half	88, 38
	約三キロ	*yaku sankiro*	approximately 3 km/kg	4

約　約　約

約　約　約

212	弓 3h	**KYŪ, yumi** – bow (for archery/violin)

| | 弓術 | *kyūjutsu* | (Japanese) archery | 187 |
| | 弓道 | *kyūdō* | (Japanese) archery | 149 |

弓　弓　弓

弓　弓　弓

213	一 亻 ノ	***SHI, ya*** – arrow
	1a2 2a 1c	弓矢　　　*yumiya*　　　bow and arrow　　　212

矢　矢　矢

矢　矢　矢

214	口 亻 一	***CHI, shi(ru)*** – know
	3d 2a 1a2	

通知　　*tsūchi*　　a notification, communication　　150
周知　　*shūchi*　　common knowledge, generally known　　91
知事　　*chiji*　　governor (of a prefecture)　　80
知人　　*chijin*　　an acquaintance　　1
知り合い　*shiriai*　　an acquaintance　　159

知　知　知

知　知　知

215 — 短

口 亻 丷 — 3d 2a 2o

***TAN, mijika(i)* – short**

長短	*chōtan*	(relative) length; good and bad points	95
短刀	*tantō*	short sword, dagger	37
短気	*tanki*	short temper, touchiness, hastiness	134
短所	*tansho*	defect, shortcoming	153
短大	*tandai*	junior college (cf. No. 449)	26

216 — 引

弓 丨 — 3h 1b

***IN, hi(ku)* – pull; attract; *hi(keru)* – be ended; make cheaper**

引力	*inryoku*	attraction, gravitation	100
引用	*in'yō*	quotation, citation	107
引き出し	*hikidashi*	drawer	53
取り引き	*torihiki*	transaction, trade	65
引き上げ	*hikiage*	raise, increase	32

217	弓 虫 ノ 3h 6d 1c	***KYŌ, GŌ, tsuyo(i)*** – strong; ***tsuyo(maru)*** – become strong(er); ***tsuyo(meru)*** – make strong(er), strengthen; ***shi(iru)*** – force

強 强力　　kyōryoku　　strength, power　　100
強国　　kyōkoku　　strong country, great power　　40
強情　　gōjō　　stubbornness, obstinacy　　209
強引に　gōin ni　　by force　　216

強　強　強

強　強　強

218	弓 冫 3h2 2b2	***JAKU, yowa(i)*** – weak; ***yowa(ru/maru)*** – become weak(er); ***yowa(meru)*** – make weak(er), weaken

弱 強弱　　kyōjaku　　strengths and weaknesses, strength　　217
弱点　　jakuten　　a weakness, weak point　　169
弱体　　jakutai　　weak　　61
弱気　　yowaki　　faintheartedness; bearishness (of market)　　134

弱　弱　弱

弱　弱　弱

219	犭虫 3g 6d	**DOKU, hito(ri)** – alone			
		独立	dokuritsu	independence	121
		独身	dokushin	unmarried, single	59
		独学	dokugaku	self-study	109
		日独	Nichi-Doku	Japan and Germany, Japanese-German	5
		和独	Wa-Doku	Japanese-German (dictionary)	124

独　独　独

独　独　独

220	匚亻一 2t 2a 1a2	**I** – medicine, healing			
		医学	igaku	medicine	109
		医学部	igakubu	medical department/school	109, 86
		医学用語	igaku yōgo	medical term	109, 107, 67
		医者	isha	physician, doctor	164
		女医	joi	woman physician, lady doctor	102

医　医　医

医　医　医

221	方 イ 一
	4h 2a 1a3

族

ZOKU – family, tribe

家族	kazoku	family	165
親族	shinzoku	relative, kin	175
一族	ichizoku	one's whole family, kin	2
部族	buzoku	tribe	86
民族	minzoku	race, people, nation	177

族　族　族

族　族　族

222	方 厂 一
	4h 2p 1a

旅

RYO, tabi – trip, travel

旅行	ryokō	trip, travel	68
旅行者	ryokōsha	traveler, tourist	68, 164
旅人	tabibito	traveler, wayfarer	1
旅先	tabisaki	destination	50
旅立つ	tabidatsu	start on a journey	121

旅　旅　旅

旅　旅　旅

223	イ 冂 2a2 2r	**NIKU** – meat, flesh

肉屋　　　*nikuya*　　　butcher (shop)　　　167
肉体　　　*nikutai*　　　the body, the flesh　　　61
肉親　　　*nikushin*　　　blood relationship/relative　　　175
肉付きのよい　*nikuzuki no yoi*　well-fleshed, plump　　　192
肉筆　　　*nikuhitsu*　　　one's own handwriting; autograph　　　130

肉　　肉　　肉

224	米 6b	**BEI, MAI, kome** – rice

白米　　　*hakumai*　　　polished rice　　　205
新米　　　*shimai*　　　new rice; novice　　　174
外米　　　*gaimai*　　　imported rice　　　83
日米　　　*Nichi-Bei*　　　Japan and America, Japanese-U.S.　　　5
南米　　　*Nanbei*　　　South America　　　74

米　　米　　米　　米　　米　　米　　米

225	女 米 女 4i 6b 3e	**SŪ, [SU], kazu** – number; **kazo(eru)** – count

数字	*sūji*	digit, numeral, figures	110
数学	*sūgaku*	mathematics	109
人数	*ninzū*	number of people	1
無数	*musū*	countless, innumerable	93
手数	*tesū*	trouble, bother	57

226	頁 米 亻 9a 6b 2a	**RUI** – kind, type, genus

親類	*shinrui*	relative, kin	175
人類	*jinrui*	mankind	1
書類	*shorui*	papers, documents	131
分類	*bunrui*	classification	38
類語	*ruigo*	synonym	67

227	一 車 ノ	**JŪ, CHŌ, omo(i)** – heavy; **kasa(naru/neru)** – lie/pile on top of one another; **-e** – -fold, -ply		
	1a 7c 1c			

体重	taijū	body weight	61
重力	jūryoku	gravity, gravitation	100
重大	jūdai	weighty, grave, important	26
二重	nijū, futae	double, twofold	3

228	禾 車 一	**SHU** – kind, type; seed; **tane** – seed; species; cause		
	5d 7c 1a			

種類	shurui	kind, type, sort	226
一種	isshu	kind, sort	2
人種	jinshu	a human race	1
種子	shushi	seed, pit	103
不安の種	fuan no tane	cause of unease	94, 105

229	、 ク	***TA, ō(i)*** – much, many, numerous					
	1d2 2n2	多少	*tashō*	much or little, many or few; some			144
		多数	*tasū*	large number (of); majority			225
		大多数	*daitasū*	the overwhelming majority			26, 225
		多元的	*tagenteki*	pluralistic			137, 210
		数多く	*kazuōku*	many, great number (of)			225

230	口	***HIN*** – refinement; article; ***shina*** – goods, quality					
	3d3	上品	*jōhin*	refined, elegant, graceful			32
		下品	*gehin*	unrefined, gross, vulgar			31
		品質	*hinshitsu*	quality			176
		部品	*buhin*	(spare/machine) parts			86
		品物	*shinamono*	merchandise			79

231	力 車 ノ 2g 7c 1c2	**DŌ, ugo(ku/kasu)** – (intr./tr.) move		
		自動車 jidōsha automobile, car		62, 133
		動物 dōbutsu animal		79
		動力 dōryoku moving force, (electric) power		100
		行動 kōdō action		68
		動員 dōin mobilize		163

動

動 動 動

動 動 動

232	イ 車 力 2a 7c 2g	**DŌ, hatara(ku)** – work		
		実働時間 jitsudōjikan actual working hours		203, 42, 43
		働き hataraki work; functioning; ability		
		働き口 hatarakiguchi job, position		54
		働き者 hatarakimono hard worker		164
		働き手 hatarakite worker, breadwinner; capable man		57

働

働 働 働

働 働 働

233	⺍ ⼧ 力 3n 2i 2g	**RŌ** – labor, toil		
		労働 rōdō work, labor		232
		労働者 rōdōsha worker, laborer		232, 164
		労働時間 rōdō jikan working hours		232, 42, 43
		労力 rōryoku trouble, effort; labor		100
		心労 shinrō worry, concern		97

労

労 労 労

労 労 労

234	十 力 2k 2g3	**KYŌ** – cooperation		
		協力 kyōryoku cooperation		100
		協力者 kyōryokusha collaborator, coworker		100, 164
		協同 kyōdō cooperation, collaboration, partnership		198
		協会 kyōkai society, association		158
		日米協会 Nichi-Bei Kyōkai the America-Japan Society		5, 224, 158

協

協 協 協

協 協 協

235	夕 力 一 4i 2g 1a2	**MU, tsuto(meru)** – work, serve

事務所　*jimusho*　office　80, 153
公務員　*kōmuin*　government employee　126, 163
国務　*kokumu*　affairs of state　40
外務省　*Gaimushō*　Ministry of Foreign Affairs　83, 145
法務省　*Hōmushō*　Ministry of Justice　123, 145

務

236	一 日 土 1a 4c 3b	**YA, no** – field, plain

野生　*yasei*　wild (animal/plant)　44
平野　*heiya*　a plain　202
　　　Hirano　(surname)
分野　*bun'ya*　field (of endeavor)　38
野原　*nohara*　field, plain　136

野

237	氵 口 十 3a 3d 2k	**KATSU** – life, activity

生活　*seikatsu*　life　44
活発　*kappatsu*　active, lively　96
活動　*katsudō*　activity　231
活用　*katsuyō*　practical use; conjugate, inflect　107
活字　*katsuji*　printing/movable type　110

活

238	言 口 十 7a 3d 2k	**WA, hanashi** – conversation, story; **hana(su)** – speak

会話　*kaiwa*　conversation　158
電話　*denwa*　telephone　108
立ち話　*tachibanashi*　chat while standing　121
話し手　*hanashite*　speaker　57
話し合う　*hanashiau*　talk over, discuss　159

話

239	売 3p 2i 2o	**BAI, u(ru)** – sell; **u(reru)** – be sold	

売店　baiten　stand, newsstand, kiosk　168
売り子　uriko　store salesclerk　103
売り手　urite　seller　57
売り切れ　urikire　sold out　39
小売り　kouri　retailing, retail　27

| 240 | 貝 7b | **kai** – shellfish (cf. No. 453) | |

貝類　kairui　shellfish (plural)　226
ほら貝　horagai　trumpet shell, conch
貝ボタン　kaibotan　shell button

| 241 | 罒貝 5g 7b | **BAI, ka(u)** – buy | |

売買　baibai　buying and selling, trade, dealing　239
買い物　kaimono　shopping, purchase　79
買い手　kaite　buyer　57
買い主　kainushi　buyer　155
買い入れる　kaiireru　purchase, stock up on　52

| 242 | 糸 6a | **SHI, ito** – thread | |

一糸まとわぬ　isshi matowanu　stark naked　2
糸口　itoguchi　end of a thread; beginning; clue　54
糸車　itoguruma　spinning wheel　133
糸目　itome　a fine thread　55
生糸　kiito　raw silk　44

243	糸 士 冖 6a 3p 2i	**ZOKU, tsuzu(ku/keru)** – (intr./tr.) continue		
		続出	zokushutsu	appear one after another	53
		続行	zokkō	continuation	68
		相続	sōzoku	succession; inheritance	146
		手続き	tetsuzuki	procedures, formalities	57
		引き続いて	hikitsuzuite	continuously, uninterruptedly	216

244	言 士 冖 7a 3p 2i	**DOKU, TOKU, [TŌ], yo(mu)** – read		
		読者	dokusha	reader	164
		読書	dokusho	reading	131
		読本	tokuhon	reader, book of readings	25
		読み物	yomimono	reading matter	79
		読み方	yomikata	reading, pronunciation (of a word)	70

245	夂 土 子 4i 3b 2c	**KYŌ, oshi(eru)** – teach; **oso(waru)** – be taught, learn		
		教室	kyōshitsu	classroom	166
		教員	kyōin	teacher, instructor; teaching staff	163
		教会	kyōkai	church	158
		回教	kaikyō	Islam, Muhammadanism	90
		教え方	oshiekata	teaching method	70

246	亠 月 ノ 2j 4b 1c	**IKU, soda(tsu)** – grow up; **soda(teru)** – raise		
		教育	kyōiku	education	245
		体育	taiiku	physical education	61
		発育	hatsuiku	growth, development	96
		生育	seiiku	growth, development	44
		育ての親	sodate no oya	foster/adoptive parent	175

247 流

氵 亠 丨
3a 2j 1b3

RYŪ – a current; style, school (of thought); **[RU], naga(reru)** – flow; **naga(su)** – pour

流通	*ryūtsū*	circulation, distribution, ventilation	150
海流	*kairyū*	ocean current	117
流行	*ryūkō*	fashion, fad, popularity	68
一流	*ichiryū*	first class	2

248 早

日 十
4c 2k

SŌ, [SA'], haya(i) – early; fast; **haya(maru)** – be hasty; **haya(meru)** – hasten

早々	*sōsō*	early, immediately	
早目に	*hayame ni*	a little early (leaving leeway)	55
早耳	*hayamimi*	quick-eared, in the know	56
手早い	*tebayai*	quick, nimble, agile	57

249 草

艹 日 十
3k 4c 2k

SŌ, kusa – grass, plants

草原	*sōgen*	grassy plain, grasslands	136
草木	*sōmoku, kusaki*	plants and trees, vegetation	22
草本	*sōhon*	herb	25
草書	*sōsho*	(cursive script form of kanji)	131
草案	*sōan*	(rough) draft	106

250 芝

艹 一 丶
3k 1a 1d

shiba – lawn

芝生	*shibafu*	lawn	44
芝草	*shibakusa*	lawn	249
人工芝	*jinkō shiba*	artficial turf	1, 139
芝居	*shibai*	stage play, theater	171
芝居小屋	*shibai-goya*	playhouse, theater	171, 27, 167

| 251 | 艹 木 亻 | *CHA, SA* – tea | | | | | | | |
| | 3k 4a 2a | | | | | | | | |

茶色 — chairo — brown — 204
茶畑 — chabatake — tea plantation — 36
茶室 — chashitsu — tea-ceremony room — 166
茶の間 — cha no ma — living room — 43
茶道 — chadō, sadō — tea ceremony — 149

| 252 | 一 艹 丨 | *SEI, SE, yo* – world, era | | | | | | | |
| | 1a 3k 1b | | | | | | | | |

二世 — nisei — second generation — 3
中世 — chūsei — Middle Ages — 28
世間 — seken — the world, public, people — 43
出世 — shusse — success in life, getting ahead — 53
世話 — sewa — taking care of, looking after — 238

| 253 | 艹 木 一 | *YŌ, ha* – leaf, foliage | | | | | | | |
| | 3k2 4a 1a | | | | | | | | |

葉書 — hagaki — postcard — 131
青葉 — aoba — green foliage — 208
言葉 — kotoba — word; language — 66
木の葉 — ko no ha — tree leaves, foliage — 22
千葉 — Chiba — (prefecture east of Tokyo) — 15

| 254 | 亻 卜 | *KA, KE, ba(keru)* – turn oneself (into); *ba(kasu)* – bewitch | | | | | | | |
| | 2a 2m | | | | | | | | |

文化 — bunka — culture — 111
化学 — kagaku — chemistry — 109
強化 — kyōka — strengthening — 219
合理化 — gōrika — rationalization, streamlining — 159, 143
化け物 — bakemono — spook, ghost, monster — 79

255	艹 亻 卜 3k 2a 2m	**KA, hana** – flower, blossom			
		草花	*kusabana*	flower, flowering plant	249
		生け花	*ikebana*	flower arranging	44
		花屋	*hanaya*	flower shop, florist	167
		花見	*hanami*	viewing cherry blossoms	63
		花火	*hanabi*	fireworks	20

256	亻 戈 2a 4n	**DAI** – generation; age; price; **TAI, ka(waru)** – represent; **ka(eru)** – replace; **yo** – generation; **shiro** – price; substitution			
		時代	*jidai*	era, period	42
		古代	*kodai*	ancient times, antiquity	172
		世代	*sedai*	generation	252
		代理	*dairi*	representation; agent	143

257	亠 夂 丨 2j 4i 1b2	**HEN, ka(waru/eru)** – (intr./tr.) change			
		変化	*henka*	change, alteration	254
		変動	*hendō*	change, fluctuation	231
		変種	*henshu*	variety, strain	228
		変人	*henjin*	an eccentric	1
		不変	*fuhen*	immutability, constancy	94

258	亠 心 丨 2j 4k 1b2	**REN, koi** – (romantic) love; **ko(u)** – be in love; **koi(shii)** – dear, fond, long for			
		恋人	*koibito*	boyfriend, girlfriend, lover	1
		恋文	*koibumi*	love letter	111
		恋心	*koigokoro*	(awakening of) love	97
		道ならぬ恋	*michi naranu koi*	forbidden love	149

259	夂 心 ⺍	**AI** – love		
	4i 4k 3n			

恋愛	ren'ai	love	258
愛情	aijō	love	209
愛国心	aikokushin	patriotic sentiment, patriotism	40, 97
愛読	aidoku	like to read	244
愛想	aisō	amiability, sociability	147

260	又 ⺍ 冖	**JU, u(keru)** – receive; **u(karu)** – pass (an exam)		
	2h 3n 2i			

受理	juri	acceptance	143
受動	judō	passive	231
受け身	ukemi	passivity; passive (in grammar)	59
受(け)付(け)	uketsuke	receptionist, reception desk	192
受け取る	uketoru	receive, accept, take	65

261	戈 一 丨	**SEI, [JŌ], na(ru)** – become; consist (of); **na(su)** – do; form		
	4n 1a 1b			

成長	seichō	growth	95
成年	seinen	(age of) majority, adulthood	45
成立	seiritsu	establishment, founding	121
合成	gōsei	composition, synthesis	159
成り行き	nariyuki	course (of events), development	68

262	心 戈 口	**KAN** – feeling, sensation		
	4k 4n 3d			

五感	gokan	the 5 senses	7
感心	kanshin	admire	97
感想	kansō	one's thoughts, impressions	147
感情	kanjō	feelings, emotion	209
感受性	kanjusei	sensibility, sensitivity	260, 98

175

263	日 耳 又 4c 6e 2h	**SAI, motto(mo)** – highest, most			
		最後	saigo	end; last	48
		最新	saishin	newest, latest	174
		最大	saidai	maximum, greatest, largest	26
		最高	saikō	maximum, highest, best	190
		最上	saijō	best, highest	32

最 最 最 最

最 最 最

264	又 厂 2h 2p	**YŪ, tomo** – friend			
		友人	yūjin	friend	1
		学友	gakuyū	fellow student, classmate; alumnus	109
		親友	shin'yū	close friend	175
		友好	yūkō	friendship	104
		友情	yūjō	friendliness, friendship	209

友 友 友 友

友 友 友

265	月 厂 4b 2p	**YŪ, U, a(ru)** – be, exist, have			
		国有	kokuyū	state-owned	40
		私有	shiyū	privately owned	125
		所有	shoyū	possession, ownership	153
		有名	yūmei	famous	82
		有力	yūryoku	influential, powerful	100

有 有 有 有

有 有 有

266	口 一 ノ 3d 1a 1c	**GŌ** – number; pseudonym			
		番号	bangō	(identification) number	185
		三号室	sangōshitsu	Room No. 3	4, 166
		年号	nengō	name/year of a reign era	45
		信号	shingō	signal	157
		号外	gōgai	an extra (edition of a newspaper)	83

号 号 号 号

号 号 号

267 別 (2f 3d 1a)

BETSU – different, separate; another, special; **waka(reru)** – diverge, part, bid farewell

区別	kubetsu	difference, distinction	183
分別	funbetsu	discretion, good judgment	38
別人	betsujin	different person	1
別居	bekkyo	(legal) separation; live separately	171

268 在 (3b 2p 1b)

ZAI – outskirts, country; be located; **a(ru)** – be, exist

所在地	shozaichi	(prefectural) capital, (country) seat; location	153, 118
在日	zainichi	(stationed) in Japan	5
在外	zaigai	overseas, abroad	83
不在	fuzai	absence	94

269 存 (2c 2p 1b)

SON, ZON – exist; know, believe

存在	sonzai	existence	268
生存	seizon	existence, life	44
存続	sonzoku	continuance, duration	243
共存	kyōson, kyōzon	coexistence	196
存分に	zonbun ni	as much as one likes, freely	38

270 麦 (4i 3b 1a)

BAKU, mugi – wheat, barley, rye, oats

小麦	komugi	wheat	27
大麦	ōmugi	barley	26
麦畑	mugibatake	wheat field	36
麦わら	mugiwara	(wheat) straw	
麦茶	mugicha	wheat tea, barley water	251

271	糸 土 一 6a 3b 1a	**SO** – element; beginning; **SU** – naked, uncovered, simple	

素質	soshitsu	nature, makeup	176
質素	shisso	simple, plain	176
元素	genso	chemical element	137
水素	suiso	hydrogen	21
素人	shirōto	amateur, layman	1

272	一 衤 1a2 5e	**HYŌ** – table, chart; surface; expression; **omote** – surface, obverse; **arawa(reru)** – be expressed; **arawa(su)** – express	

時間表	jikanhyō	timetable, schedule	42, 43
代表的	daihyōteki	representative, typical	256, 210
表情	hyōjō	facial expression	209
発表	happyō	announcement, publication	96

273	亠 衤 日 2j 5e 4c	**RI, ura** – reverse side, back, rear	

表裏	hyōri	inside and outside; double-dealing	272
裏口	uraguchi	back door, rear entrance	54
裏道	uramichi	back street; secret path	149
裏付け	urazuke	backing, support; corroboration	192
裏切る	uragiru	betray, double-cross	39

274	口 一 丨 3s 1a3 1b2	**MEN** – face, mask, surface, aspect; **omote, omo, tsura** – face	

方面	hōmen	direction, side	70
表面	hyōmen	surface, exterior	272
面会	menkai	interview, meeting	158
面目	menmoku, menboku	face, honor, dignity	55

275	├─┤ 2m 1a2 1b	**SEI, SHŌ, tada(shii)** – correct, just; **tada(su)** – correct; **masa (ni)** – just, exactly; certainly

校正	*kōsei*	proofreading	115
不正	*fusei*	injustice	94
正面	*shōmen*	front, front side	274
正月	*shōgatsu*	January; New Year	17

正 正 正

正 正 正

276	頁口 ˅ 9a 3d 2o	**TŌ, [TO], ZU, atama, kashira** – head, leader, top

後頭(部)	*kōtō(bu)*	back of the head	48, 86
出頭	*shuttō*	appearance, attendance, presence (at official proceeding)	53
先頭	*sentō*	(in the) front, lead	50
口頭	*kōtō*	oral, verbal	54
頭上	*zujō*	overhead	32

頭 頭 頭

頭 頭 頭

277	頁立 彡 9a 5b 3j	**GAN, kao** – face

顔面	*ganmen*	face	274
顔色	*kaoiro*	complexion; a look	204
素顔	*sugao*	face without makeup	271
新顔	*shingao*	stranger; newcomer	174
知らん顔	*shirankao*	pretend not to notice, ignore	214

顔 顔 顔

顔 顔 顔

278	立土 一 5b 3b 1a	**SAN** – childbirth; production; property; **u(mu)** – give birth/rise to; **u(mareru)** – be born; **ubu** – birth; infant

出産	*shussan*	childbirth, delivery	53
生産	*seisan*	production	44
産物	*sanbutsu*	product	79
不動産	*fudōsan*	immovable property, real estate	94, 231

産 産 産

産 産 産

279	⺌ 木 一 2o 4a 1a3	**GYŌ** – occupation, business, undertaking; **GŌ** – karma; **waza** – act, deed, work, art

業		
工業	*kōgyō*	industry	139
産業	*sangyō*	industry	278
事業	*jigyō*	undertaking, enterprise	80
実業家	*jitsugyōka*	businessman, industrialist	203, 165

280	犭 3g	**KEN, inu** – dog

犬		
番犬	*banken*	watchdog	185
愛犬	*aiken*	pet/favorite dog	259
野犬	*yaken*	stray dog	236
小犬	*koinu*	puppy	27
犬小屋	*inugoya*	doghouse	27, 167

281	牛 4g	**GYŪ, ushi** – cow, bull, cattle

牛		
牛肉	*gyūniku*	beef	223
野牛	*yagyū*	buffalo, bison	236
水牛	*suigyū*	water buffalo	21
小/子牛	*koushi*	calf	27, 103
牛小屋	*ushigoya*	cowshed, barn	27, 167

282	牛 土 十 4g 3b 2k	**TOKU** – special

特		
特別	*tokubetsu*	special	267
特色	*tokushoku*	distinguishing characteristic	204
特有	*tokuyū*	characteristic, peculiar (to)	265
独特	*dokutoku*	peculiar, original, unique	219
特長	*tokuchō*	strong point, forte	95

283	馬 10a	***BA, uma, [ma]*** – horse		
		馬車	*basha*	horse-drawn carriage	133
		馬力	*bariki*	horsepower	100
		馬術	*bajutsu*	horseback riding, dressage	187
		竹馬	*takeuma, chikuba*	stilts	129
		馬小屋	*umagoya*	a stable	27, 167

馬 馬 馬

馬 馬 馬
馬 馬 馬

284	駅 10a 3r 1d	***EKI*** – (train) station		
		東京駅	*Tōkyō-eki*	Tokyo Station	71, 189
		当駅	*tōeki*	this station	77
		駅前	*ekimae*	(in) front of/opposite the station	47
		駅長	*ekichō*	stationmaster	95
		駅員	*ekiin*	station employee	163

駅 駅 駅

駅 駅 駅

285	鳥 11b	***CHŌ, tori*** – bird		
		白鳥	*hakuchō*	swan	205
		野鳥	*yachō*	wild bird	236
		花鳥	*kachō*	flowers and birds	255
		一石二鳥	*isseki-nichō*	killing 2 birds with 1 stone	2, 78, 3
		鳥居	*torii*	Shinto shrine archway	171

鳥 鳥 鳥

鳥 鳥 鳥

286	島 3o 4c 1a2	***TŌ, shima*** – island		
		半島	*hantō*	peninsula	88
		島民	*tōmin*	islander	177
		無人島	*mujintō*	uninhabited island	93, 1
		島国	*shimaguni*	island country	40
		島々	*shimajima*	(many) islands	

島 島 島

島 島 島

287 一｜ノ — 1a2 1b 1c

MŌ, ke – hair, fur, feather, down

原毛	genmō	raw wool	136
毛筆	mōhitsu	brush (for writing/painting)	130
不毛	fumō	barren, sterile	94
毛糸	keito	wool yarn, knitting wool	242
まゆ毛	mayuge	eyebrow	

毛

288 䒑王 — 2o 4f

YŌ, hitsuji – sheep

羊毛	yōmō	wool	287
羊肉	yōniku	mutton	223
小/子羊	kohitsuji	lamb	27, 103

羊

289 氵王丶 — 3a 4f 2o

YŌ – ocean; foreign, Western

大洋	taiyō	ocean	26
東洋	tōyō	the East, Orient	71
西洋	seiyō	the West, Occident	72
大西洋	Taiseiyō	Atlantic Ocean	26, 72
洋書	yōsho	foreign/Western book	131

洋

290 魚 — 11a

GYO, sakana, uo – fish

魚類	gyorui	a variety of fish	226
金魚	kingyo	goldfish	23
魚肉	gyoniku	fish (meat)	223
魚市場	uoichiba	fish market	181, 154
魚屋	sakanaya	fish shop/dealer	167

魚

291	゛王 戈 2o 4f 4n	**GI** – justice, honor; meaning; in-law; artificial	
		民主主義 *minshu shugi* democracy	177, 155
		義務 *gimu* obligation, duty	235
		義理 *giri* duty, debt of gratitude	143
		同義語 *dōgigo* synonym	198, 67
		類義語 *ruigigo* word of similar meaning, synonym	226, 67

292	言 王 戈 7a 4f 4n	**GI** – deliberation; proposal	
		会議 *kaigi* conference, meeting	158
		協議 *kyōgi* council, conference	234
		議会 *gikai* parliament, diet, congress	158
		議員 *giin* M.P., dietman, congressman	163
		不思議 *fushigi* marvel, wonder, mystery	94, 99

293	言 艹 亻 7a 3k 2a	**RON** – discussion, argument; thesis, dissertation	
		論理 *ronri* logic	143
		理論 *riron* theory	143
		世論 *yoron, seron* public opinion	252
		論議 *rongi* discussion, argument	292
		論文 *ronbun* thesis, essay	111

294	王 4f	**Ō** – king	
		王国 *ōkoku* kingdom	40
		国王 *kokuō* king	40
		女王 *joō* queen	102
		王子 *ōji* prince	103
		法王 *hōō* pope	123

295	玉 丶 4f 1d	**GYOKU, tama** – gem, jewel; sphere, ball		
		玉石	gyokuseki	wheat and chaff, good and bad	78
		玉子	tamago	egg (cf. No. 1058)	103
		水玉	mizutama	drop of water	21
		目玉	medama	eyeball	55
		十円玉	jūendama	10-yen piece/coin	12, 13

玉 玉 玉

玉 玉 玉

296	宀 玉 丶 3m 4f 1d	**HŌ, takara** – treasure		
		宝石	hōseki	precious stone, gem	78
		宝玉	hōgyoku	precious stone, gem	295
		国宝	kokuhō	national treasure	40
		家宝	kahō	family heirloom	165
		宝物	hōmotsu, takaramono	treasure, prized possession	79

宝 宝 宝

宝 宝 宝

297	王 日 ノ 4f 4c 1c	**KŌ, Ō** – emperor		
		天皇	tennō	emperor	141
		皇女	kōjo	imperial princess	102
		皇居	kōkyo	imperial palace	171
		皇室	kōshitsu	imperial household	166
		皇位	kōi	imperial throne	122

皇 皇 皇

皇 皇 皇

298	王 目 丶 4f 5c 2o	**GEN** – present; **arawa(reru)** – appear; **arawa(su)** – show		
		現代	gendai	contemporary, modern	256
		現在	genzai	current, present; present tense	268
		現金	genkin	cash	23
		表現	hyōgen	an expression	272
		実現	jitsugen	realize, attain; come true	203

現 現 現

現 現 現

299	糸 6a	日 4c	氵 3a

SEN – line

光線	*kōsen*	light, light ray	138
内線	*naisen*	(telephone) extension	84
無線	*musen*	wireless, radio	93
二番線	*nibansen*	Track No. 2	3, 185
地平線	*chiheisen*	horizon	118, 202

線　線　線

線　線　線

300	⺌ 3n	日 4c	十 2k

TAN – single, simple

単語	*tango*	word	67
単位	*tan'i*	unit, denomination	122
単一	*tan'itsu*	single, simple, individual	2
単数	*tansū*	singular (in grammar)	225
単独	*tandoku*	independent, single-handed	219

単　単　単

単　単　単

301	戈 4n	日 4c	⺌ 3n

SEN, tataka(u) – wage war, fight; **ikusa** – war, battle

内戦	*naisen*	civil war	84
交戦	*kōsen*	war, warface	114
合戦	*kassen*	battle; contest	159
休戦	*kyūsen*	truce, cease-fire	60
戦後	*sengo*	postwar	48

戦　戦　戦

戦　戦　戦

302	⺈ 2n	十 2k	一 1a2

SŌ, araso(u) – dispute, argue, contend for

戦争	*sensō*	war	301
争議	*sōgi*	dispute, strife	292
論争	*ronsō*	argument, controversy	293
争点	*sōten*	point of contention, issue	169
言い争う	*iiarasou*	quarrel, argue	66

争　争　争

争　争　争

303	ク 心 一 2n 4k 1a3	**KYŪ** – urgent, sudden; *iso(gu)* – be in a hurry		
急		急行　　　*kyūkō*　　　an express (train)　　　68 特急　　　*tokkyū*　　a special express (train)　282 急変　　　*kyūhen*　　sudden change　　　257 急用　　　*kyūyō*　　　urgent business　　　107 急性　　　*kyūsei*　　　acute　　　　　　　98		

304	心 口 一 4k 3s 1a2	**AKU, O, waru(i)** – bad, evil		
悪		悪化　　　　*akka*　　　change for the worse　　254 悪性　　　　*akusei*　　malignant, vicious　　　98 悪事　　　　*akuji*　　　evil deed　　　　　　80 最悪　　　　*saiaku*　　the worst, at worst　　263 悪口　　*akkō, warukuchi*　abusive language, speaking ill of　54		

305	一 木 1a 4a	**MATSU, BATSU, sue** – end		
末		週末　　　*shūmatsu*　　weekend　　　　　　91 月末　　*getsumatsu*　　end of the month　　17 年末　　　*nenmatsu*　　year's end　　　　　45 末代　　　*matsudai*　　all ages to come, eternity　256 末っ子　　*suekko*　　youngest child　　　103		

306	一 木 1a 4a	**MI** – not yet		
未		未来　　　　*mirai*　　　future　　　　　　　69 未知　　　　*michi*　　　unknown　　　　　214 前代未聞　*zendaimimon*　unprecedented　　47, 256, 64 未満　　　　*miman*　　less than, under　　201 未明　　　　*mimei*　　early dawn, before daybreak　18		

---

307 (3d 4a 1a)

MI, aji – taste; *aji(wau)* – taste; relish, appreciate

意味	imi	meaning, significance, sense	132
正味	shōmi	net (amount/weight/price)	275
不気味	bukimi	uncanny, eerie, ominous	94, 134
地味	jimi	plain, subdued, undemonstrative	118
三味線	shamisen	samisen (3-stringed instrument)	4, 299

308 (4e 3b)

SHA – Shinto shrine; company, firm; *yashiro* – Shinto shrine

社会	shakai	society, social	158
会社	kaisha	company, firm	158
本社	honsha	our company; head office	25
社長	shachō	company president	95
社員	shain	employee, staff member	163

309 (1b 4c)

SHIN, mō(su) – say; be named

答申	tōshin	report, findings	160
上申	jōshin	report (to a superior)	32
内申	naishin	unofficial/confidential report	84
申し入れ	mōshiire	offer, proposal, notice	52
申し合わせ	mōshiawase	an understanding	159

310 (4e 4c 1b)

SHIN, JIN, kami, [kan], [kō] – god, God

神道	shintō	Shintoism	149
神社	jinja	Shinto shrine	308
神話	shinwa	myth, mythology	238
神父	shinpu	(Catholic) priest, Father	113
神風	kamikaze	divine wind; kamikaze	29

311

一 亻 ノ
1a2 2a 1c

SHITSU, ushina(u) – lose

失業	shitsugyō	unemployment	279
失意	shitsui	disappointment, despair	132
失神	shisshin	faint, lose consciousness	310
失恋	shitsuren	unrequited love	258
見失う	miushinau	lose sight of	63

失

失 失 失

失 失 失

312

金 亻 一
8a 2a 1a2

TETSU – iron

鉄道	tetsudō	railroad	149
地下鉄	chikatetsu	subway	118, 31
私鉄	shitetsu	private railway	125
鉄かぶと	tetsukabuto	steel helmet	

鉄

鉄 鉄 鉄

鉄 鉄 鉄

313

金 日 ノ
8a 4c 1c

GIN – silver

銀行	ginkō	bank	68
日銀	Nichigin	the Bank of Japan	5
銀色	gin'iro	silver color	204
水銀	suigin	mercury	21
銀メダル	ginmedaru	silver medal	

銀

銀 銀 銀

銀 銀 銀

314

木 日 ノ
4a 4c 1c

KON – root; perseverance; **ne** – root, base, origin

大根	daikon	daikon, Japanese radish	26
根本的	konponteki	fundamental; radical	25, 210
根気	konki	patience, perseverance	134
屋根	yane	roof	167
根強い	nezuyoi	deep-rooted, firmly established	217

根

根 根 根

根 根 根

315	一 イ 1a2 2a	**FU, [FŪ], otto** – husband, man			
		夫人	fujin	wife, Mrs.	1
		人夫	ninpu	laborer	1
		水夫	suifu	sailor, seaman	21
		工夫	kōfu	laborer	139
			kufū	contrivance, scheme, means	

夫　夫　夫

夫夫夫

316	女 巾 ⼧ 3e 3f 2i	**FU** – woman, wife			
		夫婦	fūfu	husband and wife, married couple	315
		主婦	shufu	housewife	155
		婦人	fujin	lady, woman	1
		婦女 (子)	fujo(shi)	woman	102, 103
		婦長	fuchō	head nurse	95

婦　婦　婦

婦婦婦

317	リ 巾 ⼧ 2f 3f 2i	**KI, kae(ru)** – return; **kae(su)** – let return, dismiss			
		帰国	kikoku	return to one's country	40
		帰宅	kitaku	return/come/get home	178
		帰路	kiro	the way home	151
		帰化	kika	become naturalized	254
		日帰り	higaeri	go and return in a day	5

帰　帰　帰

帰帰帰

318	十 又 2k 2h	**SHI** – branch; support; **sasa(eru)** – support			
		支出	shishutsu	expenditure, disbursement	53
		支社	shisha	branch (office)	308
		支店	shiten	branch office/store	168
		支部	shibu	branch, local chapter	86
		支流	shiryū	tributary (of a river)	247

支　支　支

支支支

319	米 十 、 6b 2k 1d2	**RYŌ** – materials; fee

料理　　　*ryōri*　　　cooking, cuisine; dish, food　　143
原料　　　*genryō*　　raw materials　　136
料金　　　*ryōkin*　　fee, charge, fare　　23
手数料　　*tesūryō*　　fee; commission　　57, 225
有/無料　　*yū/muryō*　　pay, toll, charging a fee/free　　265, 93

料　料　料

料　料　料

320	禾 十 、 5d 2k 1d2	**KA** – academic course, department, faculty

科学　　　　　*kagaku*　　　science　　109
理科　　　　　*rika*　　　　natural science (department)　　143
外科　　　　　*geka*　　　　surgery　　93
産婦人科医　　*sanfujinkai*　gynecologist　　278, 316, 1, 220
教科書　　　　*kyōkasho*　　textbook, schoolbook　　245, 131

科　科　科

科　科　科

321	一 日 丨 (1a) 4c 1b	**RYŌ, yo(i)** – good

良好　　*ryōkō*　　　good, favorable, satisfactory　　104
良質　　*ryōshitsu*　　good quality　　176
最良　　*sairyō*　　　best　　263
不良　　*furyō*　　　bad, unsatisfactory; delinquency　　94
良心　　*ryōshin*　　conscience　　97

良　良　良

良　良　良

322	食 8b	**SHOKU, [JIKI]** – food; eating; **ta(beru), ku(u/rau)** – eat

食事　　　*shokuji*　　　meal, dinner　　80
食料品　　*shokuryōhin*　food, foodstuffs　　319, 230
和/洋食　　*wa/yō-shoku*　Japanese/Western food　　124, 289
夕食　　　*yūshoku*　　　evening meal, supper　　81
食べ物　　*tabemono*　　food　　79

食　食　食

食　食　食

323 飠欠 8b 4j

IN, no(mu) – drink

飲食	inshoku	food and drink, eating and drinking	322
飲料	inryō	drink, beverage	319
飲料水	inryōsui	drinking water	319, 21
飲み水	nomimizu	drinking water	21
飲み物	nomimono	(something to) drink, beverage	79

324 厂又 2p 2h

HAN, [HON] – anti-; *[TAN]* – (unit of land/cloth measurement); *so(ru/rasu)* – (intr./tr.) warp, bend back

反発	hanpatsu	repulsion, repellence; opposition	96
反日	han-Nichi	anti-Japanese	5
反面	hanmen	the other side	274
反省	hansei	reflection, introspection; reconsideration	145

325 飠厂又 8b 2p 2h

HAN, meshi – cooked rice; meal, food

ご飯	gohan	cooked rice; meal, food	
赤飯	sekihan	(festive) rice boiled with red beans	207
夕飯	yūhan, yūmeshi	evening meal, supper, dinner	81
飯ごう	hangō	mess kit, eating utensils	
飯場	hanba	construction camp/bunkhouse	154

326 宀口 3m 3d2

KAN – government, authorities

半官半民	hankan-hanmin	semigovernmental	88, 177
国務長官	kokumu chōkan	secretary of state	40, 235, 95
外交官	gaikōkan	diplomat	83, 114
高官	kōkan	high government official/office	190
神官	shinkan	Shinto priest	310

327 館
食 宀 口
8b 3m 3d2

KAN – (large) building, hall

旅館	*ryokan*	Japanese-style inn	222
水族館	*suizokukan*	aquarium	22, 221
会館	*kaikan*	(assembly) hall	158
本館	*honkan*	main building	25
別館	*bekkan*	annex, extension	267

328 管
竹 宀 口
6f 3m 3d2

KAN – pipe; wind instrument; control; *kuda* – pipe, tube

管内	*kannai*	(area of) jurisdiction	84
管理	*kanri*	administration, supervision	143
水道管	*suidōkan*	water pipe/conduit	21, 149
気管	*kikan*	windpipe, trachea	134
鉄管	*tekkan*	iron tube/pipe	312

329 利
禾 刂
5d 2f

RI – advantage; (loan) interest; *ki(ku)* – take effect, work

有利	*yūri*	profitable, advantageous	265
利子	*rishi*	interest (on a loan)	103
利用	*riyō*	make use of	107
利口	*rikō*	smart, clever, bright	54
左利き	*hidarikiki*	left-hander	75

330 便
亻 日 一
2a 4c 1a

BEN – convenience; excrement; **BIN** – opportunity; mail; *tayo(ri)* – news, tidings

便利	*benri*	convenient, handy	329
不便	*fuben*	inconvenient	94
便所	*benjo*	toilet	153
別便	*betsubin*	separate mail	267

331 | 亻 口 一 | (2a) (3s) (1a)

SHI – use; messenger; *tsuka(u)* – use

大 使	*taishi*	ambassador	26
公 使	*kōshi*	minister, envoy	126
天 使	*tenshi*	angel	141
使 用 法	*shiyōhō*	how to use, directions for use	107, 123
使 い 方	*tsukaikata*	how to use, way to handle	70

使　使　使

使　使　使

332 | 一 口 丨 | (1a) (3s) (1b)

SHI – history, chronicles

日 本 史	*nihonshi*	Japanese history	5, 25
中 世 史	*chūseishi*	medieval history	28, 252
文 学 史	*bungakushi*	history of literature	111, 109
史 実	*shijitsu*	historical fact	203
女 史	*joshi*	(honorific) Madame, Miss, Mrs.	102

史　史　史

史　史　史

333 | 亻 士 | (2a) (3p)

SHI, [JI], tsuka(eru) – serve

仕 事	*shigoto*	work, job	80
仕 立 て 屋	*shitateya*	tailor; dressmaker	121, 167
仕 方	*shikata*	way, method, means	70
仕 手	*shite*	protagonist, leading role (in Noh)	57
仕 上 げ る	*shiageru*	finish up, complete	32

仕　仕　仕

仕　仕　仕

334 | 亻 士 ノ | (2a) (3p) (1c)

NIN – duty, responsibility, office; *maka(seru/su)* – entrust (to)

主 任	*shunin*	person in charge, manager, head	155
信 任	*shinnin*	confidence, trust	157
後 任	*kōnin*	successor	48
任 務	*ninmu*	duty, office, mission	235
任 意	*nin'i*	optional, voluntary	132

任　任　任

任　任　任

335	木 隹 一 4a 8c 1a2	**KEN, [GON]** – authority, power; right

権利	*kenri*	a right	329
人権	*jinken*	human rights	1
特権	*tokken*	special right, privilege	282
主権	*shuken*	sovereignty	155
三権分立	*sanken bunritsu*	separation of powers	4, 38, 121

権

権　権　権

権　権　権

336	木 口 又 4a 3d 2h	**KYOKU** – end, pole; **GOKU** – very, extremely; *kiwa(mi)* – height, end; *kiwa(meru/maru)* – carry to/reach its end

北/南極	*hok/nan-kyoku*	north/south pole	73, 74
極東	*kyokutō*	the Far East	71
極上	*gokujō*	finest, top quality	32
見極める	*mikiwameru*	see through, discern	63

極

極　極　極

極　極　極

337	口 一 ノ 3d 1a 1c	**KU** – phrase, sentence, verse

語句	*goku*	words and phrases	67
成句	*seiku*	set phrase, idiom	261
文句	*monku*	words, expression; objection	111
句読点	*kutōten*	punctuation mark	244, 169
引用句	*in'yōku*	quotation	216, 107

句

句　句　句

句　句　句

338	日 一 ノ 4c 1a 1c	**JUN** – 10-day period

上旬	*jōjun*	first 10 days of a month (1st to 10th)	32
中旬	*chūjun*	second 10 days of a month (11th to 20th)	28
下旬	*gejun*	last third of a month (21st to end)	31

旬

旬　旬　旬

旬　旬　旬

339	図 口 ノ 丶 3s 1c 1d3	*ZU* – drawing, diagram, plan; *TO, haka(ru)* – plan	
		地図 *chizu* map	118
		図表 *zuhyō* chart, table, graph	272
		合図 *aizu* signal, sign, gesture	159
		意図 *ito* intention	132
		図書館 *toshokan* library	131, 327

340	計 言 十 7a 2k	*KEI* – measuring; plan; total; *haka(ru)* – measure, compute; *haka(rau)* – arrange, dispose of, see about	
		時計 *tokei* clock, watch	42
		会計 *kaikei* accounting; paying a bill	158
		合計 *gōkei* total	159
		家計 *kakei* household finances	165

341	針 金 十 8a 2k	*SHIN, hari* – needle	
		方針 *hōshin* course, line, policy	70
		針路 *shinro* course (of a ship)	151
		長/分針 *chō/funshin* minute hand	95, 38
		短針 *tanshin* hour hand	215
		針金 *harigane* wire	23

342	調 言 土 口 7a 3b 3d	*CHŌ, shira(beru)* – investigate, check; *totono(eru)* – prepare, arrange, put in order; *totono(u)* – be prepared, arranged	
		強調 *kyōchō* cooperation, harmony	234
		好調 *kōchō* good, favorable	104
		調子 *chōshi* tone; mood; condition	103
		取り調べ *torishirabe* investigation, questioning	65

343 一 日 丨
1a 4c 1b3

GA – picture; *KAKU* – stroke (in writing kanji)

画家	gaka	painter	165
日本/洋画	nihon/yō-ga	Japanese/Western-style painting	5, 25, 289
画用紙	gayōshi	drawing paper	107, 180
画面	gamen	(TV/movie/computer) screen	274
計画	keikaku	plan, project	340

画 画 画

画 画 画

344 氵 日 宀
3a 4c 3m

EN – performance, presentation, play

上演	jōen	performance, dramatic presentation	32
公演	kōen	public performance	126
独演	dokuen	solo performance	219
出演	shutsuen	appearance, performance	53
演出	enshutsu	production, staging (of a play)	53

演 演 演

演 演 演

345 糸 亻 一
6a 2a 1a2

KAI, E – picture

絵画	kaiga	pictures, paintings, drawings	343
絵葉書	ehagaki	picture postcard	253, 131
絵本	ehon	picture book	25
口絵	kuchie	frontispiece	54
大和絵	Yamato-e	ancient Japanese-style painting	26, 124

絵 絵 絵

絵 絵 絵

346 糸 口 亻
6a 3d 2a

KYŪ – supply

給料	kyūryō	pay, wages, salary	319
月給	gekkyū	monthly salary	17
支給	shikyū	supply, provisioning, allowance	318
供給	kyōkyū	supply	197
給水	kyūsui	water supply	21

給 給 給

給 給 給

347	立 5b	日 4c	**ON, IN, oto, ne** – sound		
			発音	*hatsuon*	pronunciation	96
			表音文字	*hyōon moji*	phonetic symbol	272, 111, 110
			母音	*boin*	vowel	112
			本音	*honne*	one's true intention	25
			足音	*ashioto*	sound of footsteps	58

音

348	日 4c2	立 5b	**AN, kura(i)** – dark, dim		
			暗黒	*ankoku*	darkness	206
			暗室	*anshitsu*	darkroom	166
			暗号	*angō*	(secret) code, cipher	266
			明暗	*meian*	light and darkness, shading	18
			暗がり	*kuragari*	darkness	

暗

349	貝 7b	立 5b	日 4c	**IN** – rhyme		
				音韻学	*on'ingaku*	phonology	347, 109
				韻文	*inbun*	verse, poetry	111
				韻語	*ingo*	rhyming words	67
				頭韻	*tōin*	alliteration	276

韻

350	扌 3c	貝 7b	口 3d	**SON** – loss, damage; **soko(nau/neru)** – harm, injure; **-soko(nau)** – fail to, err in		
				損失	*sonshitsu*	loss	311
				大損	*ōzon*	great loss	26
				見損なう	*misokonau*	miss (seeing); misjudge	63
				読み損なう	*yomisokonau*	misread	244

損

351 一 冂 亻 (1a) 2r 2a

Ō – center, middle

中央	chūō	center	28
中央口	chūōguchi	main/middle exit	28, 54
中央部	chūōbu	central part, middle	28, 86
中央線	Chūō-sen	the Chuo (train) Line	28, 299
中央区	Chūō-ku	Chuo Ward (Tokyo)	28, 183

352 日 冂 亻 4c 2r 2a

EI, *utsu(su)* – reflect, project; *utsu(ru)* – be reflected, projected; *ha(eru)* – shine, be brilliant

映画	eiga	movie	343
反映	han'ei	reflection	324
上映	jōei	showing, screening (of a movie)	32
夕映え	yūbae	the glow of sunset	81

353 艹 冂 亻 3k 2r 2a

EI – brilliant, talented, gifted

英気	eiki	energetic spirit, enthusiasm	134
石英	sekiei	quartz	78
英語	Eigo	the English language	67
和英	Wa-Ei	Japanese-English	124
英会話	Eikaiwa	English conversation	158, 238

354 頁 日 卜 9a 4c 2m

DAI – topic, theme; title

問題	mondai	problem, question	162
議題	gidai	topic for discussion, agenda	292
話題	wadai	topic	238
表題	hyōdai	title, caption	272
宿題	shukudai	homework	179

| 355 | 宀 卜 亻
3m 2m 2a | **TEI, JŌ, sada(meru)** – determine, decide; **sada(maru)** – be determined, decided; **sada(ka)** – certain, definite |

安定	*antei*	stability, equilibrium	105
協定	*kyōtei*	agreement, pact	234
定食	*teishoku*	meal of fixed menu, complete meal	322
未定	*mitei*	undecided, unsettled, not yet fixed	306

| 356 | 氵 亻 一
3a 2a 1a2 | **KETSU, ki(meru)** – decide; **ki(maru)** – be decided |

決定	*kettei*	decision, determination	355
決心	*kesshin*	determination, resolution	97
決意	*ketsui*	determination, resolution	132
議決	*giketsu*	decision (of a committee)	292
未決	*miketsu*	pending	306

| 357 | 氵 王 丶
3a 4f 1d | **CHŪ** – note, comment; **soso(gu)** – pour, flow |

注意	*chūi*	attention, caution, warning	132
注目	*chūmoku*	attention, notice	55
注文	*chūmon*	order, commission	111
発注	*hatchū*	order, commission	96
注入	*chūnyū*	injection; pour into, infuse	52

| 358 | 艹 日 冫
4a 4c 2b | **GAKU** – music; **RAKU** – pleasure; **tano(shimu)** – enjoy; **tano(shii)** – fun, enjoyable, pleasant |

音楽	*ongaku*	music	347
文楽	*bunraku*	Japanese puppet theater	111
楽天家	*rakutenka*	optimist	141, 165
安楽死	*anrakushi*	euthanasia	105, 85

359	艹 日 木 3k 4c 4a	*YAKU, kusuri* – medicine			
		薬学	*yakugaku*	pharmacy	109
		薬品	*yakuhin*	medicines, drugs	230
		薬味	*yakumi*	spices	307
		薬局	*yakkyoku*	pharmacy	170
		薬屋	*kusuriya*	drugstore, pharmacy	167

薬

360	亻 ト 一 2a 2m 1a2	*SAKU, SA, tsuku(ru)* – make			
		作家	*sakka*	writer	165
		作品	*sakuhin*	(literary) work, work (of art), opus	230
		作戦	*sakusen*	military operation, tactics	301
		作り話	*tsukuribanashi*	made-up story, fabrication	238
		手作り	*tezukuri*	handmade	57

作

361	日 ト 一 4c 2m 1a2	*SAKU* – past, yesterday			
		昨年	*sakunen*	last year	45
		昨日	*sakujitsu, kinō*	yesterday	5
		一昨日	*issakujitsu, ototoi*	day before yesterday	2, 5
		一昨年	*issakunen, ototoshi*	year before last	2, 45
		昨今	*sakkon*	these days, recent	51

昨

362	几 又 ト 2s 2h 2m	*DAN* – step; stairs; rank; column			
		一段	*ichidan*	step; single-stage	2
		石段	*ishidan*	stone stairway	78
		段々畑	*dandanbatake*	terraced fields	36
		手段	*shudan*	means, measure	57
		段取り	*dandori*	program, plan, arrangements	65

段

363	一 日 丨 (1a) 4c 1b	***YU, YŪ, [YUI], yoshi*** – reason, cause; significance

由来 *yurai* origin, derivation 69
理由 *riyū* reason, grounds 143
自由 *jiyū* freedom 62
不自由 *fujiyū* discomfort; want, privation 94, 62
事由 *jiyū* reason, cause 80

由

由

364	氵 日 丨 3a 4c 1b	***YU, abura*** – oil

石油 *sekiyu* oil, petroleum 78
原油 *gen'yu* crude oil 136
油田 *yuden* oil field 35
給油所 *kyūyusho, kyūyujo* filling/gas station 346, 153
油絵 *aburae* oil painting 345

油

油

365	亠 十 ノ 2j 2k 1c	***TAI*** – against; ***TSUI*** – pair

反対 *hantai* opposite; opposition 324
対立 *tairitsu* confrontation 121
対決 *taiketsu* showdown 356
対面 *taimen* interview, meeting 274
対話 *taiwa* conversation, dialogue 238

対

対

366	一 日 丨 (1a) 4c 1b2	***KYOKU*** – curve; melody, musical composition; ***ma(geru)*** – bend, distort; ***ma(garu)*** – (intr.) bend, turn

作曲 *sakkyoku* musical composition 360
名曲 *meikyoku* famous/well-known melody 82
曲線 *kyokusen* a curve 299
曲がり道 *magarimichi* winding street 149

曲

曲

367	⸜ ⾋ 冂			
	2o 3k 2r			

TEN – law code; ceremony

古典	koten	classical literature, the classics	172
百科事典	hyakkajiten	encyclopedia	14, 320, 80
法典	hōten	code of laws	123
出典	shutten	literary source, authority	53
特典	tokuten	special favor, privilege	282

368	⸜ 口 冂			
	2o 3d 2r			

KŌ, KYŌ – interest; entertainment; liveliness; prosperity; *oko(ru)* – flourish, prosper; *oko(su)* – revive, retrieve

興行	kōgyō	entertainment industry; performance	68
興信所	kōshinjo	private inquiry/detective agency	157, 153
興業	kōgyō	industrial enterprise	279
興味	kyōmi	interest	307

369	厂 日 一			
	2p 4c 1a2			

NŌ – agriculture

農業	nōgyō	agriculture	279
農村	nōson	farm village	191
農民	nōmin	farmer, peasant	177
農家	nōka	farmhouse, farm household; farmer	165
農産物	nōsanbutsu	agricultural product	278, 79

370	一 丨			
	1a2 1b			

KO, KI, onore – self

自己	jiko	self-	62
自己中心	jiko chūshin	egocentric	62, 28, 97
利己	riko	selfishness, egoism	329
利己的	rikoteki	selfish, self-centered	329, 210
知己	chiki	acquaintance	214

371 記

言 一 丨
7a 1a2 1b

KI, shiru(su) – write/note down

記者	kisha	newspaperman, journalist	164
記事	kiji	article, report	80
日記	nikki	diary	5
暗記	anki	memorize	348
記号	kigō	mark, symbol	266

372 紀

糸 一 丨
6a 1a2 1b

KI – narrative, history

紀元	kigen	era (of year reckoning)	137
紀元前/後	kigen-zen/go	B.C./A.D.	137, 47, 48
世紀	seiki	century	252
紀行 (文)	kikō(bun)	account of a journey	68, 111
風紀	fūki	discipline, public morals	29

373 起

土 卜 イ
3b 2m 2a

KI – awakening, rise, beginning; **o(kiru)** – get/wake/be up; **o(koru)** – occur; **o(kosu)** – give rise; wake (someone) up

起原	kigen	origin, beginning	136
起点	kiten	starting point	169
早起き	hayaoki	get up early	248
起き上がる	okiagaru	get up, pick oneself up	32

374 得

彳 日 十
3i 4c 2k

TOKU – profit, advantage; **e(ru), u(ru)** – gain, acquire

損得	sontoku	profit and loss	350
所得	shotoku	income	153
得点	tokuten	one's score, points made	169
得意	tokui	prosperity; pride; one's strong point	132
心得る	kokoroeru	know, understand	97

375	彳 几 又 3i 2s 2h	**YAKU** – service, use; office, post; **EKI** – battle; service		
		役所	*yakusho*	government office/bureau	153
		役人	*yakunin*	public official	1
		役員	*yakuin*	(company) officer, director	163
		役者	*yakusha*	player, actor	164
		使役	*shieki*	employment, service	331

役

376	舟 口 丶 6c 3d 2o	**SEN, fune, [funa]** – ship		
		船長	*senchō*	captain	95
		船員	*sen'in*	crewman, seaman, sailor	163
		船室	*senshitsu*	cabin	166
		汽船	*kisen*	steamship, steamer	135
		船旅	*funatabi*	sea voyage	222

船

377	广 艹 又 3q 3k 2h	**DO, [TAKU], [TO]** – degree, measure, limit; times; **tabi** – times		
		一度	*ichido*	once; 1 degree (of temperature/arc)	2
		今度	*kondo*	this time; soon; next time	51
		年度	*nendo*	business/fiscal year	45
		高度成長	*kōdo seichō*	high growth	190, 261, 95
		支/仕度	*shitaku*	preparations	318, 333

度

378	氵 厂 艹 3a 2p 3k	**TO, wata(ru)** – cross; **wata(su)** – hand over		
		渡来	*torai*	introduction (into); visit	69
		渡し船	*watashibune*	ferryboat	376
		渡り鳥	*wataridori*	migratory bird	285
		見渡す	*miwatasu*	look out over	63
		手渡す	*tewatasu*	hand deliver, hand over	57

渡

379	广 3q 艹 3k 巾 3f	**SEKI** – seat, place	

出席 shusseki attendance 53
満席 manseki full, fully occupied 201
議席 giseki seat (in parliament) 292
主席 shuseki top seat, head, chief 155
席上 sekijō (at) the meeting; (on) the occasion 32

380	广 5i 冂 2r 亻 2a	**BYŌ, [HEI], ya(mu)** – fall ill, suffer from; **yamai** – illness	

病気 byōki sickness, disease 134
重病 jūbyō serious illness 227
急病 kyūbyō sudden illness 303
性病 seibyō venereal disease 98
病人 byōnin sick person 1

381	心 4k2 立 5b 日 4c	**OKU** – remember, think	

記憶 kioku memory, recollection 371
憶病 okubyō cowardice, timidity 380

382	亻 2a 立 5b 日 4c	**OKU** – 100 million	

一億 ichioku 100 million 2
億万長者 okuman chōja multimillionaire 16, 95, 164
数億年 sūokunen hundreds of millions of years 225, 45

383	欠 4j	**KETSU, ka(ku)** – lack; **ka(keru)** – be lacking	
		欠点　　　*ketten*　　　defect, flaw	169
		出欠　　　*shukketsu*　　attendance (and/or absence)	53
		欠席　　　*kesseki*　　　absence, nonattendance	379
		欠員　　　*ketsuin*　　　vacant position, opening	163
		欠損　　　*kesson*　　　deficit, loss	350

384	冫 2b 欠 4j	**JI, SHI, tsugi** – next; **tsu(gu)** – come/rank next	
		次官　　　*jikan*　　　vice-minister	326
		次男　　　*jinan*　　　second-oldest son	101
		二次　　　*niji*　　　second, secondary	3
		目次　　　*mokuji*　　　table of contents	55
		相次ぐ　　*aitsugu*　　follow/happen one after another	146

385	耳 6e 立 5b 戈 4n	**SHOKU** – employment, job, occupation, office	
		職業　　　*shokugyō*　　occupation, profession	279
		職場　　　*shokuba*　　place of work, jobsite	154
		職員　　　*shokuin*　　personnel, staff, staff member	163
		現職　　　*genshoku*　　one's present post	298
		無職　　　*mushoku*　　unemployed	93

386	月 4b ヒ 2m2 ノ 1c	**NŌ** – ability, function; Noh play	
		能力　　　*nōryoku*　　capacity, talent	100
		本能　　　*honnō*　　instinct	25
		能筆　　　*nōhitsu*　　calligraphy, skilled penmanship	130
		能楽　　　*nōgaku*　　Noh play	358
		能面　　　*nōmen*　　Noh mask	274

387	心 月 卜 4k 4b 2m2	**TAI** – condition, appearance		
態		態 度	*taido*	attitude	377
		生 態	*seitai*	mode of life, ecology	44
		変 態	*hentai*	metamorphosis; abnormality	257
		事 態	*jitai*	situation, state of affairs	80
		実 態	*jittai*	actual conditions/situation	203

態 態 態

388	口 一 丨 3d 1a 1b	**KA** – good; possible; approval		
可		可 能 (性)	*kanō(sei)*	possibility	386, 98
		不 可 能	*fukanō*	impossible	94, 386
		不 可 欠	*fukaketsu*	indispensable, essential	94, 383
		不 可 分	*fukabun*	indivisible	94, 38
		可 決	*kaketsu*	approval (of a proposed law)	356

可 可 可

389	氵 口 一 3a 3d 1a	**KA, kawa** – river		
河		河 川	*kasen*	rivers	33
		河 口	*kakō, kawaguchi*	mouth of a river	54
		大 河	*taiga*	large river	26
		銀 河	*ginga*	the Milky Way	313
		河 原	*kawara*	dry riverbed	136

河 河 河

390	亻 口 一 2a 3d 1a	**KA, nani, [nan]** – what, which, how many		
何		何 事	*nanigoto*	what, whatever	80
		何 曜 日	*nan(i)yōbi*	what day of the week	19, 5
		何 日	*nannichi*	how many days; what day of the month	5
		何 時	*nanji*	what time	42
		何 時 間	*nanjikan*	how many hours	42, 43

何 何 何

391	艹 口 亻 3k 3d 2a	**KA, ni** – load, cargo, baggage

在 荷	zaika	stock, inventory	268
入 荷	nyūka	fresh supply/arrival of goods	52
出 荷	shukka	shipment, shipping	53
(手) 荷 物	(te)nimotsu	(hand)baggage, luggage	57, 79
重 荷	omoni	heavy burden	227

荷　荷　荷

荷 荷 荷

392	欠 口 一 4j 3d2 1a2	**KA, uta** – poem, song; **uta(u)** – sing

歌 手	kashu	singer	57
国 歌	kokka	national anthem	40
和 歌	waka	31-syllable Japanese poem	124
短 歌	tanka	(synonym for waka)	215
流 行 歌	ryūkōka	popular song	247, 68

歌　歌　歌

歌 歌 歌

393	一 丨 丶 1a2 1b 1d	**YO** – previously, in advance

予 約	yoyaku	subscription, reservation, booking	211
予 定	yotei	plan; expectation	355
予 想	yosō	expectation, supposition	147
予 知	yochi	foresee, predict	214
予 言	yogen	prophecy, prediction	66

予　予　予

予 予 予

394	頁 一 丨 9a 1a2 1b	**YO, azu(keru/karu)** – entrust/receive for safekeeping

預 金	yokin	deposit, bank account	23
預 かり 所	azukarisho, azukarijo	depository, warehouse	153
手 荷 物 一 時 預 かり (所)	tenimotsu ichiji azukari(sho/jo) (place for) temporary handbaggage storage		57, 391, 79, 2, 42, 153

預　預　預

預 預 預

395	彡 艹 一 3j 3k 1a	**KEI, GYŌ, katachi, kata** – form, shape		
		円形	*enkei*	round/circular shape	13
		正方形	*seihōkei*	square	275, 70
		無形	*mukei*	formless, immaterial, intangible	93
		人形	*ningyō*	doll, puppet	1
		手形	*tegata*	(bank) bill, note, draft	57

396	門 艹 一 8e 3k 1a	**KAI** – opening, development; *a(ku/keru)* – (intr./tr.) open; *hira(keru)* – become developed; *hira(ku)* – (tr.) open		
		公開	*kōkai*	open to the public	126
		開会	*kaikai*	opening of a meeting	158
		未開	*mikai*	uncivilized, backward, savage	306
		開発	*kaihatsu*	development	96

397	門 十 ノ 8e 2k 1c	**HEI, shi(meru), to(jiru/zasu)** – close, shut; *shi(maru)* – become closed		
		開閉	*kaihei*	opening and closing	396
		閉会	*heikai*	closing, adjournment	158
		閉店	*heiten*	store closing	168
		閉口	*heikō*	be dumbfounded	54

398	門 ヅ 亻 8e 2o 2a	**KAN, seki** – barrier		
		関門	*kanmon*	gateway, barrier	161
		関心	*kanshin*	interest	97
		関東	*Kantō*	(region including Tokyo)	71
		関西	*Kansai*	(region including Osaka and Kyoto)	72
		関所	*sekisho*	barrier station, checkpoint	153

399	禾口 丶丶 5d 3d 2o2	**ZEI** – tax			
		税金	zeikin	tax	23
		所得税	shotokuzei	income tax	153, 374
		関税	kanzei	customs, duty, tariff	398
		税関	zeikan	customs, customshouse	398
		無税	muzei	tax-free, duty-free	93

税

400	言口 丶丶 7a 3d 2o2	**SETSU** – opinion, theory; **ZEI, to(ku)** – explain; persuade			
		説明	setsumei	explanation	18
		社説	shasetsu	an editorial	308
		小説	shōsetsu	novel, story	27
		演説	enzetsu	a speech	344
		説教	sekkyō	sermon	245

説

401	丶丶王亻 2o 4f 2a	**BI, utsuku(shii)** – beautiful			
		美術館	bijutsukan	art museum/gallery	187, 327
		美学	bigaku	esthetics	109
		美人	bijin	beautiful woman	1
		美化	bika	beautification	254
		美点	biten	beauty, merit, good point	169

美

402	丶丶食王 2o 8b 4f	**YŌ, yashina(u)** – rear; adopt; support; recuperate			
		養育	yōiku	upbringing, nurture	246
		養成	yōsei	training, cultivation	261
		教養	kyōyō	culture, education	245
		養子	yōshi	adopted child	103
		休養	kyūyō	rest, recreation; recuperation	60

養

403	木 王 ⸜	***YŌ*** – way, manner; similarity; condition; ***sama*** – condition; Mr., Mrs., Miss		
	4a 4f 2o			

様子	*yōsu*	situation, aspect, appearance	103
同様	*dōyō*	same	198
多様	*tayō*	diversity, variety	229
神様	*kamisama*	God	310
田中明様	*Tanaka Akira sama*	Mr. Akira Tanaka	35, 28, 18

404	⸜ 弓 |	***DAI*** – (prefix for ordinals), degree		
	6f 3h 1b			

第一	*daiichi*	No. 1; first, best, main	2
毎月第二土曜日	*maitsuki daini doyōbi*	second Saturday of every month	
		116, 17, 3, 24, 19, 5	
第三者	*daisansha*	third person/party	4, 164
次第	*shidai*	sequence; circumstances; as soon as	384

405	⸜ 弓 |	***TEI, [DAI], [DE], otōto*** – younger brother		
	2o 3h 1b			

義弟	*gitei*	younger brother-in-law	291
子弟	*shitei*	sons, children	103
弟子	*deshi*	pupil, apprentice, disciple	103
門弟	*montei*	pupil, follower	161
弟分	*otōtobun*	like a younger brother	38

406	口 ⸜	***KEI, [KYŌ], ani*** – elder brother		
	3d 2o			

兄弟	*kyōdai*	brothers, brothers and sisters	405
父兄	*fukei*	parents and brothers; guardians	113
義兄	*gikei*	elder brother-in-law	291
実兄	*jikkei*	one's brother by blood	203
兄さん	*niisan*	elder brother	

407	女 巾 亠 3e 3f 2j	**SHI, ane** – elder sister		
		義姉	*gishi*	elder sister-in-law	291
		姉さん	*nēsan*	elder sister; young lady	

姉　姉　姉

姉　姉　姉

408	女 未 一 3e 4a 1a	**MAI, imōto** – younger sister		
		姉妹	*shimai*	sisters	407
		姉妹都市	*shimai toshi*	sister cities	407, 188, 181
		弟妹	*teimai*	younger brothers and sisters	405
		義妹	*gimai*	younger sister-in-law	291

妹　妹　妹

妹　妹　妹

409	巾 口 一 3f 3d2 1a	**SHI** – teacher; army		
		教師	*kyōshi*	teacher, instructor	245
		医師	*ishi*	physician	220
		法師	*hōshi*	Buddhist priest	123
		山師	*yamashi*	speculator; adventurer; charlatan	34
		師弟	*shitei*	master and pupil	405

師　師　師

師　師　師

410	立 日 土 5b 4c 3b	**DŌ, warabe** – child		
		学童	*gakudō*	schoolchild	109
		童話	*dōwa*	nursery story, fairy tale	238
		童顔	*dōgan*	childlike/boyish face	277
		童心	*dōshin*	child's mind/feelings	97
		神童	*shindō*	child prodigy	310

童　童　童

童　童　童

411	日 土 一 4c2 3b 1a	**RYŌ** – quantity; **haka(ru)** – (tr.) measure, weigh

大/小 量　　tai/shōryō　　large/small quantity　　26, 144
雨 量　　uryō　　(amount of) rainfall　　30
大量生産　tairyō seisan　mass production　26, 44, 278
分 量　　bunryō　　quantity, amount; dosage　　38
重 量　　jūryō　　weight　　227

412	亠 口 ヽ 2j 3d 2o2	**SHŌ, akina(u)** – deal (in), trade

商 人　　shōnin　　merchant, dealer　　1
商 品　　shōhin　　goods, merchandise　　230
商 業　　shōgyō　　commerce, business　　279
商 売　　shōbai　　trade, business; one's trade　　239
商 工　　shōkō　　commerce and industry　　139

413	辶 口 冂 2q 3d 2r2	**KA, su(giru)** – pass, exceed, too much; **su(gosu)** – spend (time); **ayama(tsu)** – err; **ayama(chi)** – error

過 度　　kado　　excessive, too much　　377
通 過　　tsūka　　passage, transit　　150
過半数　kahansū　majority, more than half　88, 225
食べ過ぎる　tabesugiru　eat too much, overeat　322

414	土 ノ ヽ 3b 1c 1d	**KYO, KO, sa(ru)** – leave, move away; pass, elapse

去 年　　kyonen　　last year　　45
死 去　　shikyo　　death　　85
去 来　　kyorai　　coming and going　　69
過 去　　kako　　past　　413
立ち去る　tachisaru　leave, go away　　121

415	辶 口 亠 2q 3d 2j	**TEKI** – fit, be suitable			
		適当	tekitō	suitable, appropriate	77
		適度	tekido	to a proper degree, moderate	377
		適切	tekisetsu	pertinent, appropriate	39
		適用	tekiyō	application (of a rule)	107
		適合	tekigō	conformity, compatibility	159

416	夂 口 亠 4i 3d 2j	**TEKI, kataki** – enemy, opponent, competitor			
		宿敵	shukuteki	old/hereditary enemy	179
		強敵	kyōteki	powerful foe, formidable rival	217
		敵意	tekii	enmity, hostility	132
		敵対	tekitai	hostility, antagonism	365
		不敵	futeki	fearless, daring	94

417	禾 王 口 5d 4f 3d	**TEI, hodo** – degree, extent			
		程度	teido	degree, extent, grade	377
		過程	katei	a process	413
		工程	kōtei	progress of the work; manufacturing process	139
		日程	nittei	schedule for the day	5
		音程	ontei	musical interval, step	347

418	糸 冂 一 6a 2r 1a3	**SO, kumi** – group, crew, class, gang; **ku(mu)** – put together			
		組成	sosei	composition, makeup	261
		番組	bangumi	(TV) program	185
		労働組合	rōdō kumiai	labor union	233, 232, 159
		組み立て	kumitate	construction; assembling	121
		組み合わせる	kumiawaseru	combine, fit together	159

419	女 口 一 3e 3s 1a	**YŌ** – main point, necessity; **i(ru)** – need, be necessary		
		重要	*jūyō*	important	227
		主要	*shuyō*	principal, major	155
		要点	*yōten*	main point, gist	169
		要素	*yōso*	element, factor	271
		要約	*yōyaku*	summary	211

要

420	目 丷 一 5c 2o 1a	**GU** – tool		
		具体的	*gutaiteki*	concrete, specific	61, 210
		道具	*dōgu*	tool, implement	149
		家具	*kagu*	furniture	165
		金具	*kanagu*	metal fitting	23
		不具	*fugu*	deformity, crippled	94

具

421	亻 口 一 2a 3s 1a	**KA, atai** – price, value		
		物価	*bukka*	price (of commodities)	79
		米価	*beika*	price of rice	224
		単価	*tanka*	unit price	300
		定価	*teika*	fixed/list price	355
		現金正価	*genkin seika*	cash price	298, 23, 275

価

422	十 目 丷 2k 5c 2o	**SHIN** – truth, genuineness, reality; **ma** – true, pure, exactly		
		真実	*shinjitsu*	the truth, a fact	203
		真理	*shinri*	truth	143
		真相	*shinsō*	the truth, the facts	146
		真空	*shinkū*	vacuum	140
		真っ暗	*makkura*	pitch-dark	348

真

423 　十 目 丨
2k 5c 1b

CHOKU, JIKI – honest, frank, direct; **nao(su)** – fix, correct; **nao(ru)** – be fixed, corrected; **tada(chi ni)** – immediately

直線	chokusen	straight line	299
直前/後	choku-zen/go	immediately before/after	47, 48
正直	shōjiki	honest, upright	275
書き直す	kakinaosu	write over again, rewrite	131

直

424 　木 目 十
4a 5c 2k

SHOKU, u(eru) – plant; **u(waru)** – be planted

植物	shokubutsu	a plant	79
動植物	dōshokubutsu	animals and plants	231, 79
植民地	shokuminchi	colony	177, 118
植木	ueki	garden/potted plant	22
田植え	taue	rice planting	35

植

425 　亻 目 十
2a 5c 2k

CHI, ne, atai – value, price

価値	kachi	value	421
値うち	neuchi	value; public estimation	
値段	nedan	price	362
値上げ	neage	price increase	32
値切る	negiru	haggle over the price, bargain	39

値

426 　罒 目 十
5g 5c 2k

CHI, o(ku) – put, set; leave behind/as is

位置	ichi	position, location	122
置き物	okimono	ornament; figurehead	79
物置き	monooki	storeroom, shed	79
前置き	maeoki	introductory remarks, preface	47
一日置き	ichinichioki	every other day	2, 5

置

427 制 — 刂 巾 一 (2f 3f 1a2)

SEI – system; regulations

制 度	seido	system	377
税 制	zeisei	system of taxation	399
新 制	shinsei	new order, reorganization	174
強 制	kyōsei	compulsion, force	217
管 制	kansei	control	328

428 製 — ネ 巾 刂 (5e 3f 2f)

SEI – produce, manufacture, make

製 作	seisaku	a work, production	360
製 品	seihin	product	230
製 鉄	seitetsu	iron manufacturing	312
木 製	mokusei	wooden, made of wood	22
日 本 製	nihonsei	Japanese-made, Made in Japan	5, 25

429 走 — 土 卜 亻 (3b 2m 2a)

SŌ, hashi(ru) – run

走 路	sōro	(race) track, course	151
走 行 時 間	sōkō jikan	travel time	68, 42, 43
走 り 回 る	hashirimawaru	run around	90
走 り 書 き	hashirigaki	flowing/hasty handwriting	131
口 走 る	kuchibashiru	babble, blurt out	54

430 徒 — 彳 土 卜 (3i 3b 2m)

TO – on foot; companions; vain, useless

生 徒	seito	pupil, student	44
教 徒	kyōto	believer, adherent	245
使 徒	shito	apostle	331
徒 手	toshu	empty-handed; penniless	57
徒 労	torō	vain effort	233

431

ソ　ト　一
3n　2m　1a

HO, BU, [FU], aru(ku), ayu(mu) – walk

歩道	hodō	footpath, sidewalk	149
歩行者	hokōsha	pedestrian	68, 164
一歩	ippo	a step	2
歩調	hochō	pace, step	342
歩合	buai	rate, percentage; commission	159

432

氵　ソ　ト
3a　3n　2m

SHŌ – cross over; have to do with

| 交渉 | kōshō | negotiations | 114 |

433

車　一　ノ
7c　1a2　1c

TEN, koro(bu/garu/geru) – roll over, fall down; **koro(gasu)** – roll, knock down

自転車	jitensha	bicycle	62, 133
回転	kaiten	rotation, revolution	90
空転	kūten	idling (of an engine)	140
転任	tennin	transfer of assignments/personnel	334

434

イ　一　ノ
2a　1a2　1c

DEN, tsuta(eru) – transmit, impart; **tsuta(waru)** – be transmitted, imparted; **tsuta(u)** – go along

伝記	denki	biography	371
伝説	densetsu	legend, folklore	400
伝動	dendō	evangelism, missionary work	149
手伝い	tetsudai	help, helper	57

435	艹 一 丿 3k 1a2 1c	*GEI* – art, craft			
		芸者	*geisha*	geisha	164
		芸術	*geijutsu*	art	187
		文芸	*bungei*	literary art, literature	111
		演芸	*engei*	performance, entertainment	344
		民芸	*mingei*	folkcraft	177

436	隹 木 8c 4a	*SHŪ, atsu(maru/meru)* – (intr./tr.) gather; *tsudo(u)* – (intr.) gather			
		集金	*shūkin*	bill collecting	23
		集中	*shūchū*	concentration	28
		全集	*zenshū*	the complete works	89
		特集	*tokushū*	special edition	282
		万葉集	*Man'yōshū*	(Japan's oldest anthology of poems)	16, 253

437	辶 隹 2q 8c	*SHIN, susu(mu)* – advance, progress; *susu(meru)* – advance, promote			
		進歩	*shinpo*	progress, improvement	431
		進行	*shinkō*	progress, onward movement	68
		前進	*zenshin*	advance, forward movement	47
		先進国	*senshinkoku*	developed/advanced country	50, 40

438	冖 車 2i 7c	*GUN* – army, troops, war			
		軍人	*gunjin*	soldier, military man	1
		軍事	*gunji*	military affairs, military	80
		海軍	*kaigun*	navy	117
		敵軍	*tekigun*	enemy army/troops	416
		軍国主義	*gunkoku shugi*	militarism	40, 155, 291

439	辶 車 宀 2q 7c 2i	**UN** – fate, luck; **hako(bu)** – carry, transport	
		運転手	untenshu	driver, chauffeur	433, 57
		(労働) 運動	(rōdō) undō	(labor) movement	233, 232, 231
		運動不足	undōbusoku	lack of exercise	231, 94, 58
		運河	unga	canal	389
		不運	fuun	misfortune	94

運 運 運 運 運

440	辶 車 2q 7c	**REN** – group, accompaniment; **tsu(reru)** – take (someone); **tsura(naru)** – stand in a row; **tsura(neru)** – link, put in a row	
		連続	renzoku	series, continuity	243
		連合	rengō	combination, league, coalition	159
		国連	kokuren	United Nations	40
		家族連れ	kazokuzure	with the family	165, 221

連 連 連 連 連

441	辶 ゛ 亻 2q 2o 2a	**SŌ, oku(ru)** – send	
		運送	unsō	transport, shipment	439
		回送	kaisō	forwarding	90
		送金	sōkin	remittance	23
		送別会	sōbetsukai	going-away/farewell party	267, 158
		見送る	miokuru	see (someone) off; escort	63

送 送 送 送 送

442	辶 厂 又 2q 2p 2h	**HEN, kae(ru/su)** – (intr./tr.) return	
		返事	henji	reply	80
		返信用葉書	henshin'yō hagaki	reply postcard	157, 107, 253, 131
		見返す	mikaesu	look back; triumph over (an old enemy)	63
		読み返す	yomikaesu	reread	244
		送り返す	okurikaesu	send back	441

返 返 返 返 返

443

土 厂 又
3b 2p 2h

HAN, saka – slope, hill

急 な 坂	kyū na saka	steep slope/hill	303
坂 道	sakamichi	road on a slope	149
上 り 坂	noborizaka	ascent	32
下 り 坂	kudarizaka	descent; decline	31
赤 坂	Akasaka	(area of Tokyo)	207

444

辶 丷 屮
2q 2o 3o

GYAKU – reverse, inverse, opposite; treason; **saka** – reverse, inverse; **saka(rau)** – be contrary (to)

逆 転	gyakuten	reversal	433
逆 説	gyakusetsu	paradox	400
反 逆	hangyaku	treason	324
逆 立 つ	sakadatsu	stand on end	121

445

辶 厂 一
2q 2p 1a

KIN, chika(i) – near, close

近 所	kinjo	vicinity, neighborhood	153
付 近	fukin	vicinity, environs	192
最 近	saikin	recent; most recent, latest	263
近 代	kindai	modern times, modern	256
近 道	chikamichi	shortcut, shorter way	149

446

辶 土 口
2q 3b 3d

EN, [ON], tō(i) – far, distant

遠 方	enpō	great distance, (in) the distance	70
遠 近 法	enkinhō	(law of) perspective	445, 123
遠 足	ensoku	excursion, outing	58
遠 心 力	enshinryoku	centrifugal force	97, 100
遠 回 し	tōmawashi	indirect, roundabout	90

447 園 口 土 口
3s 3b 3d

EN, sono – garden

公園	kōen	(public) park	126
動物園	dōbutsuen	zoo	231, 79
植物園	shokubutsuen	botanical garden	424, 79
学園	gakuen	educational institution, academy	109
楽園	rakuen	paradise	358

448 達 辶 王 土
2q 4f 3b

TATSU – reach, arrive at

上達	jōtatsu	progress; proficiency	32
発達	hattatsu	development	96
達成	tassei	achieve, attain	261
達人	tatsujin	expert, master	1
友達	tomodachi	friend	264

449 期 月 艹 丷
4b 3k 2o

KI, [GO] – time, period, term

期間	kikan	period of time, term	43
定期	teiki	fixed period	355
過渡期	katoki	transition period	413, 378
学期	gakki	semester, trimester, school term	109
短期大学	tanki daigaku	junior college	215, 26, 109

450 基 土 艹 丷
3b 3k 2o

KI, moto, motoi – basis, foundation, origin

基本	kihon	basis, fundamentals; standard	25
基金	kikin	fund, endowment	23
基地	kichi	(military) base	118
基石	kiseki	foundation stone, cornerstone	78
基調	kichō	keynote	342

451	扌 土 十 3c 3b 2k	**JI, mo(tsu)** – have, possess; hold, maintain

支持	*shiji*	support	318
持続	*jizoku*	continuance, maintenance	243
持ち主	*mochinushi*	owner, possessor	155
金持ち	*kanemochi*	rich person	23
気持ち	*kimochi*	mood, feeling	134

452	彳 土 十 3i 3b 2k	**TAI, ma(tsu)** – wait for

期待	*kitai*	expectation, anticipation	449
特待	*tokutai*	special treatment, distinction	282
待ち合い室	*machiaishitsu*	waiting room	159, 166
待ち合わせる	*machiawaseru*	wait for (as previously arranged)	159
待ちぼうけ	*machibōke*	getting stood up	

453	亻 丨 2a 1b2	**KAI** – shellfish (cf. No. 240); be in between, mediate

介入	*kainyū*	intervention	52
介在	*kaizai*	lie/stand/come between	268
魚介	*gyokai*	fish and shellfish, marine products	290
一介の	*ikkai no*	mere, only	2

454	田 亻 丨 5f 2a 1b2	**KAI** – world

世界	*sekai*	world	252
世界史	*sekaishi*	world history	252, 332
学界	*gakkai*	academic world	109
外界	*gaikai*	external world, outside	83
下界	*gekai*	this world, the earth below	31

455	扌 口 刂
	3c 3d 2f

SHŌ, mane(ku) – beckon to, invite, cause

| 招待 | shōtai | invitation | 452 |
| 手招き | temaneki | beckoning | 57 |

456	糸 口 刂
	6a 3d 2f

SHŌ – introduction

| 紹介 | shōkai | introduction, presentation | 453 |
| 自己紹介 | jiko shōkai | introduce oneself | 62, 370, 453 |

457	宀 艹 氵
	3m 3k 2o

KAN – coldest season, coldness; **samu(i)** – cold

寒気	kanki	the cold	134
寒中	kanchū	the cold season	28
極寒	gokkan	severe cold	336
寒村	kanson	poor/lonely village	191
寒空	samuzora	wintry sky, cold weather	140

458	糸 夂 丶
	6a 4i 1d2

SHŪ, o(waru/eru) – come/bring to an end

最終	saishū	last	263
終戦	shūsen	end of the war	301
終点	shūten	end of the line, last stop, terminus	169
終身	shūshin	for life, lifelong	59
終日	shūjitsu	all day long	5

459	夂 、 4i 1d2	**TŌ, fuyu** – winter		
		立冬	*rittō*	first day of winter	121
		真冬	*mafuyu*	midwinter, the dead of winter	422
		冬向き	*fumuki*	for winter	199
		冬物	*fuyumono*	winter clothing	79
		冬空	*fuyuzora*	winter sky	140

冬

460	日 亻 一 4c 2a 1a3	**SHUN, haru** – spring		
		春分 (の 日)	*shunbun (no hi)*	vernal equinox	38, 5
		立春	*risshun*	beginning of spring	121
		青春	*seishun*	springtime of life, youth	208
		売春	*baishun*	prostitution	239
		春画	*shunga*	obscene picture, pornography	343

春

461	夂日 一 4i 5c 1a	**KA, [GE], natsu** – summer		
		夏期	*kaki*	the summer period	449
		立夏	*rikka*	beginning of summer	121
		真夏	*manatsu*	midsummer, height of summer	422
		夏物	*natsumono*	summer clothing	79
		夏休み	*natsuyasumi*	summer vacation	60

夏

462	禾 火 5d 4d	**SHŪ, aki** – fall, autumn		
		春夏秋冬	*shunkashūtō*	all the year round	460, 461, 459
		春秋	*shunjū*	spring and autumn; years, age	460
		秋分 (の 日)	*shūbun (no hi)*	autumnal equinox	38, 5
		秋気	*shūki*	the autumn air	134
		秋風	*akikaze*	autumn breeze	29

秋

463

即   卩日丶   2e 4c 1d

SOKU – immediately; conform (to); namely, i.e.

即時	sokuji	instantly, immediately, on the spot	42
即日	sokujitsu	on the same day	5
即金	sokkin	cash; payment in cash	23
即席	sokuseki	extemporaneous, impromptu	379
即興	sokkyō	improvised, ad-lib	368

464

節   ⺮日卩   6f 4c 2e

SETSU, [SECHI] – season; occasion; section, paragraph; verse; *fushi* – joint, knuckle; melody; point

時節	jisetsu	time of year; the times	42
調節	chōsetsu	adjustment, regulation	342
使節	shisetsu	envoy, mission	331
節約	setsuyaku	economizing, thrift	211

465

季   禾子   5d 2c

KI – season

季節	kisetsu	season, time of year	464
四季	shiki	the 4 seasons	6
季節風	kisetsufū	seasonal wind, monsoon	464, 29
季節外れ	kisetsuhazure	out of season	464, 83
季語	kigo	word indicating the season (in haiku)	67

466

委   禾女   5d 3e

I – entrust

委任	inin	trust, mandate, authorization	334
委員	iin	committee member	163
委員会	iinkai	committee	163, 158

467	氵 3a	月 4b	日 3d

KO, mizuumi – lake

湖水	kosui	lake	21
火口湖	kakōko	crater lake	20, 54
湖面	komen	surface of a lake	274
山中湖	Yamanaka-ko	(lake near Mt. Fuji)	34, 28
十和田湖	Towada-ko	(lake in Tohoku)	12, 124, 35

468	氵 3a	月 4b	日 4c

CHŌ, shio – tide; salt water; opportunity

満潮	manchō	high tide	201
潮流	chōryū	tidal current; trend of the times	247
風潮	fūchō	tide; tendency, trend	29
潮時	shiodoki	favorable tide; opportunity	42
黒潮	Kuroshio	Japan Current	206

469	月 4b	日 4c	十 2k2

CHŌ – morning; dynasty; **asa** – morning

朝食	chōshoku	breakfast	322
平安朝	Heianchō	Heian period (794-1185)	202, 105
朝日	asahi	morning/rising sun	5
毎朝	maiasa	every morning	116
今朝	kesa, konchō	this morning	51

470	日 4c	尸 3r	一 1a

CHŪ, hiru – daytime, noon

昼食	chūshoku	lunch	322
白昼に	hakuchū ni	in broad daylight	205
昼飯	hirumeshi	lunch	325
昼間	hiruma	daytime	43
昼休み	hiruyasumi	lunch break, noon recess	60

471	亠 亻 夕	**YA, yoru, yo** – night		
	2j 2a 2n	昼夜	chūya	day and night	470

471 亠亻夕 (2j 2a 2n)

YA, yoru, yo – night

昼夜	chūya	day and night	470
今夜	kon'ya	tonight	51
夜行	yakō	traveling by night; night train	68
夜学	yagaku	evening class	109
夜明け	yoake	dawn, daybreak	18

夜 夜 夜 夜

夜 夜 夜

472 氵亠亻 (3a 2j 2a)

EKI – liquid, fluid

液体	ekitai	liquid, fluid	61
液化	ekika	liquefaction	254
だ液	daeki	saliva	

液 液 液 液

液 液 液

473 宀土冂 (2n 3b 2r)

KAKU – angle, corner; **kado** – corner, angle; **tsuno** – horn, antlers

角度	kakudo	degrees of an angle, angle	377
三角 (形)	sankaku(kei)	triangle	4, 395
直角	chokkaku	right angle	423
街角	machikado	street corner	186

角 角 角 角

角 角 角

474 牛土宀 (4g 3b 2n)

KAI, GE, to(ku) – untie; solve; **to(keru)** – come loose; be solved; **to(kasu)** – comb

理解	rikai	understanding	143
解説	kaisetsu	explanation, commentary	400
解決	kaiketsu	solution, settlement	356
和解	wakai	compromise	124
解任	kainin	dismissal, release	304

解 解 解 解

解 解 解

475	艹 米 一		*KIKU* – chrysanthemum			
	3k 6b 1a					

白菊	*shiragiku*	white chrysanthemum	205
菊の花	*kiku no hana*	chrysanthemum	255
菊作り	*kikuzukuri*	chrysanthemum growing	360
菊人形	*kikuningyō*	chrysanthemum doll	1,395
菊地	*Kikuchi*	(surname)	118

476	米 冂 亻		*Ō, oku* – interior			
	6b 2r 2a					

奥義	*ōgi, okugi*	secrets, hidden mysteries	291
奥行き	*okuyuki*	depth (vs. height and width)	68
山奥	*yamaoku*	deep in the mountains	34
奥付け	*okuzuke*	colophon	192
奥さん	*okusan*	wife; ma'am	

477	卜 一 丨		*SHI, to(maru/meru)* – come/bring to a stop			
	2m 1a 1b					

終止	*shūshi*	termination, end	458
休止	*kyūshi*	pause, suspension	60
通行止め	*tsūkōdome*	Road Closed, No Thoroughfare	150, 68
口止め料	*kuchidomeryō*	hush money	54, 319
足止め	*ashidome*	keep indoors, confinement	58

478	米 卜 一		*SHI, ha* – tooth			
	6b 2m 1a					

門/犬歯	*mon/kenshi*	incisor/canine	161, 280
義歯	*gishi*	false teeth, dentures	291
歯科医	*shikai*	dentist	319, 220
歯医者	*haisha*	dentist	220, 164
歯車	*haguruma*	toothed wheel, gear	133

479	戈 ⸚ 卜	***SAI*** – year, years old; *[SEI]* – year		
	4n 3n 2m	満 四 歳	*man'yonsai*	4 (full) years old	201, 6

SAI – year, years old; *[SEI]* – year

満 四 歳	*man'yonsai*	4 (full) years old	201, 6
二 十 歳	*hatachi*	20 years old	3, 12
万 歳	*banzai*	Hurrah! Long live...!	16
歳 月	*saigetsu*	time, years	17
歳 入 歳 出	*sainyū-saishutsu*	yearly revenue and expenditure	52, 53

480	厂 木 卜	***REKI*** – continuation, passing of time
	2p 4a2 2m	

REKI – continuation, passing of time

歴 史	*rekishi*	history	332
学 歴	*gakureki*	school career, academic background	109
前 歴	*zenreki*	one's personal history, background	47
歴 任	*rekinin*	successive holding of various posts	334

481	亻 卜 一	***KI, kuwada(teru)*** – plan, undertake, attempt
	2a 2m 1a	

KI, kuwada(teru) – plan, undertake, attempt

企 業	*kigyō*	enterprise, undertaking	279
中 小 企 業	*chūshō kigyō*	small- and medium-size enterprises	28, 27, 279
企 画	*kikaku*	planning, plan	343
企 図	*kito*	plan, project, scheme	339

482	衤 木	***KIN*** – prohibition
	4e 4a2	

KIN – prohibition

禁 止	*kinshi*	prohibition	477
解 禁	*kaikin*	lifting of a ban	474
禁 制	*kinsei*	prohibition, ban	427
禁 物	*kinmotsu*	forbidden things, taboo	79
発 禁	*hakkin*	prohibition of sale	96

483	攵 卜 一 4i 2m 1a	***SEI, [SHŌ], matsurigoto*** – government, rule

政 局	*seikyoku*	political situation	170
行 政	*gyōsei*	administration	68
内 政	*naisei*	domestic politics, internal affairs	84
市 政	*shisei*	municipal government	181
家 政	*kasei*	management of a household, housekeeping	165

政　政　政

484	言 卜 一 7a 2m 1a2	***SHŌ*** – proof, evidence, certificate

証 明	*shōmei*	proof, testimony, corroboration	18
証 人	*shōnin*	witness	1
証 言	*shōgen*	testimony	66
反 証	*hanshō*	counterproof, counterevidence	324
内 証	*naisho, naishō*	secret	84

証　証　証

485	糸 士 口 6a 3p 3d	***KETSU, musu(bu)*** – tie, bind; conclude (a contract); bear (fruit); ***yu(waeru)*** – tie; ***yu(u)*** – do up (one's hair)

結 論	*ketsuron*	conclusion	293
結 成	*kessei*	formation, organization	261
結 合	*ketsugō*	union, combination	159
終 結	*shūketsu*	conclusion, termination	458

結　結　結

486	扌 立 攵 3c 5b 3e	***SETSU*** – touch, contact; ***tsu(gu)*** – join together

直 接	*chokusetsu*	direct	423
間 接	*kansetsu*	indirect	43
面 接	*mensetsu*	interview	274
接 続	*setsuzoku*	connection, joining	243
接 待	*settai*	reception, welcome; serving, offering	452

接　接　接

| 487 | 一 日 木
(1a) 4c 4a | **KA** – fruit; result; **ha(tasu)** – carry out, complete; **ha(teru)** – come to an end; **ha(te)** – end, limit; result |

結果	kekka	result	485
成果	seika	result	261
果実	kajitsu	fruit	203
果物	kudamono	fruit	79

果

果	果	果							
果	果	果							

| 488 | 言 日 木
7a 4c 4a | **KA** – lesson; section |

第一課	daiikka	Lesson 1	404, 2
課目	kamoku	subject (in school)	55
課程	katei	course, curriculum	417
課長	kachō	section chief	95
人事課	jinjika	personnel section	1, 80

課

課	課	課							
課	課	課							

| 489 | イ 木 口
2a 4a 3d | **HO, tamo(tsu)** – keep, preserve, maintain |

保証	hoshō	guarantee, warranty	484
保証人	hoshōnin	guarantor, sponsor	484, 1
保存	hozon	preservation	269
保育所	hoikusho, hoikujo	daycare nursery	246, 153
保養所	hoyōsho, hoyōjo	sanatorium, rest home	402, 153

保

保	保	保							
保	保	保							

| 490 | 宀 十 丶
3m 2k 1d | **SHU, [SU], mamo(ru)** – protect; obey, abide by; **mori** – babysitter, (lighthouse) keeper |

保守的	hoshuteki	conservative	489, 210
子守	komori	baby-sitting; baby-sitter, nursemaid	103
子守歌	komoriuta	lullaby	103, 392
見守る	mimamoru	keep watch over; stare at	63
お守り	omamori	charm, amulet	

守

守	守	守							
守	守	守							

491	口 十 丶 3s 2k 1d	**DAN, [TON]** – group	
		団体 (旅行) *dantai (ryokō)* group (tour)	61, 222, 68
		集団 *shūdan* group, mass	436
		団地 *danchi* public housing development/complex	118
		団結 *danketsu* unity, solidarity	485
		師団 *shidan* (army) division	409

492	口 ノ 丶 3d 1c 1d	**DAI, TAI** – stand, pedestal, platform, plateau	
		台所 *daidokoro* kitchen	153
		天文台 *tenmondai* observatory	141, 111
		高台 *takadai* high ground, a height	190
		台本 *daihon* script, screenplay, libretto	25
		台風 *taifū* typhoon	29

493	氵 口 ノ 3a 3d 1c	**JI, CHI** – peace; government; healing; *osa(meru)* – govern; suppress; *osa(maru)* – be at peace, quelled; *nao(ru/su)* – (intr./tr.) heal	
		政治 *seiji* politics	483
		自治 *jichi* self-government, autonomy	62
		明治時代 *Meiji jidai* Meiji era (1868–1912)	18, 42, 256

494	女 口 ノ 3e 3d 1c	**SHI, haji(maru/meru)** – (intr./tr.) start, begin	
		始末 *shimatsu* circumstances; management, disposal	305
		始終 *shijū* from first to last, all the while	458
		始発 *shihatsu* the first (train) departure	96
		開始 *kaishi* beginning, opening	396
		原始的 *genshiteki* primitive, original	136, 210

495 — 党

3n 3d 2i

TŌ – party, faction

政党	seitō	political party	483
野党	yatō	party out of power, the opposition	236
党員/首	tōin/shu	party member/leader	163, 148
徒党	totō	confederates, clique, conspiracy	430
社会党	Shakaitō	Socialist Party	308, 158

496 — 堂

3n 3d 3b

DŌ – temple; hall

食堂	shokudō	dining hall, restaurant	322
能楽堂	nōgakudō	Noh theater	386, 358
公会堂	kōkaidō	public hall, community center	126, 158
本堂	hondō	main temple	25
国会議事堂	kokkai gijidō	Diet Building	40, 158, 292, 80

497 — 常

3n 3d 3f

JŌ, tsune – normal, usual, continual; **toko-** – ever-, always

日常生活	nichijō seikatsu	everyday life	5, 44, 237
正常	seijō	normal	275
通常	tsūjō	ordinary, usual	150
常任委員	jōnin iin	member of a standing committee	334, 466, 163

498 — 非

(1a5) 2m 1b

HI – mistake; (prefix) non-, un-

非常口	hijōguchi	emergency exit	497, 54
非常事態	hijō jitai	state of emergency	497, 80, 387
非公開	hikōkai	not open to the public, private	126, 396
非人間的	hiningenteki	inhuman, impersonal	1, 43, 210
非合法	higōhō	illegal	159, 123

499

掌 ⺌ 口 扌
3n 3d 3c

SHŌ – palm of the hand; administer

合掌	gasshō	clasp one's hands (in prayer)	159
掌中	shōchū	pocket (edition), in the hand	28
掌中の玉	shōchū no tama	apple of one's eye, one's jewel	28, 295
車掌	shashō	(train) conductor	133

500

賞 ⺌ 貝 口
3n 7b 3d

SHŌ – prize; praise

文学賞	bungaku-shō	prize for literature	111, 109
ノーベル賞	Nōberu-shō	Nobel Prize	
賞品	shōhin	a prize	230
賞金	shōkin	cash prize, prize money	23
受賞者	jushōsha	prizewinner	260, 164

501

束 一 木 口
(1a) 4a 3s

SOKU, taba – bundle, sheaf

一束	issoku, hitotaba	a bundle	2
約束	yakusoku	promise, appointment	211
結束	kessoku	unity, union, bond	485
花束	hanataba	bouquet	255
束ねる	tabaneru	tie in a bundle; control	

502

速 辶 木 口
2q 4a 3s

SOKU, haya(i), sumi(yaka) – fast, quick, prompt; **haya(meru)** – quicken, accelerate

速力/度	soku-ryoku/do	speed, velocity	100, 377
高速道路	kōsoku dōro	expressway, freeway	190, 149, 151
速達	sokutatsu	special/express delivery	448
速記	sokki	shorthand, stenography	371

503

整 | 攵 木 口
4i | 4a | 3s

SEI, *totono(eru)* – put in order, prepare; ***totono(u)*** – be put in order, prepared

整理	*seiri*	arrangement, adjustment	143
調整	*chōsei*	adjustment, modulation	342
整形外科	*seikei geka*	plastic surgery	395, 83, 320
整数	*seisū*	integer	225

504

府 | 广 イ 十
3q | 2a | 2k

FU – storehouse; government office; capital city

政府	*seifu*	government	483
無政府	*museifu*	anarchy	93, 483
首府	*shufu*	the capital	148
京都府	*Kyōto-fu*	Kyoto Prefecture	189, 188
都道府県	*todōfuken*	the Japanese prefectures	188, 149, 194

505

符 | ⺮ イ 十
6f | 2a | 2k

FU – sign, mark; amulet

切符	*kippu*	ticket	39
切符売り場	*kippu uriba*	ticket office/window	39, 239, 154
音符	*onpu*	diacritical mark; musical note	347
符号	*fugō*	mark, symbol	266
符合	*fugō*	coincidence, agreement, correspondence	159

506

券 | 一 刂 イ
1a2 | 2f | 2a

KEN – ticket, certificate

入場券	*nyūjōken*	admission ticket	52, 154
旅券	*ryoken*	passport	222
回数券	*kaisūken*	coupon ticket	90, 225
定期券	*teikiken*	commutation ticket, (train) pass	355, 449
(有価)証券	*(yūka) shōken*	securities	265, 421, 484

507	一 亅 丨
	1a4 2a 1b

KAN, maki – roll, reel; volume; **ma(ku)** – roll, wind

上/中/下 巻	jō/chū/ge-kan	first/middle/last volume	32, 28, 31
第 一 巻	daiikkan	Volume 1	404, 2
絵 巻 (物)	emaki(mono)	picture scroll	345, 79
葉 巻	hamaki	cigar	253
取 り 巻 く	torimaku	surround, encircle	65

508	囗 亻 一
	3s 2a 1a4

KEN – circle, range, sphere

共 産 圏	kyōsanken	the Communist bloc/countries	196, 278
極 地 圏	kyokuchiken	polar region	336, 118
北/南 極 圏	hok/nan-kyokuken	Arctic/Antarctic Circle	73, 74, 336
首 都 圏	shutoken	the capital region	148, 188
圏 内/外	kennai/gai	within/outside the range (of)	84, 83

509	月 力 亻
	4b 2g 2a

SHŌ, ka(tsu) – win; **masa(ru)** – be superior (to)

勝 利	shōri	victory	329
勝 (利) 者	shō(ri)sha	victor, winner	329, 164
決 勝	kesshō	decision (of a competition)	356
連 勝	renshō	series of victories, winning streak	440
勝 ち 通 す	kachitōsu	win successive victories	150

510	宀 貝
	2n 7b

FU, ma(keru) – be defeated, lose; give a discount; **ma(kasu)** – beat, defeat; **o(u)** – carry, bear; owe

勝 負	shōbu	victory or defeat; game, match	509
自 負	jifu	conceit, self-importance	62
負 け ん 気	makenki	unyielding/competitive spirit	134
負 け 犬	makeinu	loser	280

511 貝 攵 7b 4i

HAI, yabu(reru) – be defeated, beaten, frustrated

敗北	*haiboku*	defeat	73
勝敗	*shōhai*	victory or defeat, outcome	509
失敗	*shippai*	failure, blunder	311
敗戦	*haisen*	lost battle, defeat	301
敗者	*haisha*	the defeated, loser	164

512 方 攵 4h 4i

HŌ, hana(tsu) – set free, release; fire (a gun); emit; **hana(su)** – set free, release; **hana(reru)** – get free of

解放	*kaihō*	liberation, emancipation	474
放送	*hōsō*	(radio/TV) broadcasting	441
放火	*hōka*	arson	20
放置	*hōchi*	let alone, leave as is, leave to chance	426

513 阝 方 2d 4h

BŌ, fuse(gu) – defend/protect from, prevent

防止	*bōshi*	prevention, keeping in check	477
予防	*yobō*	prevention, precaution	393
国防	*kokubō*	national defense	40
防火	*bōka*	fire prevention/fighting	20
防水	*bōsui*	waterproof, watertight	21

514 攵 一 丨 4i 1a2 1b

KAI, arata(meru) – alter, renew, reform; **arata(maru)** – be altered, renewed, corrected

改正	*kaisei*	improvement; revision	275
改良	*kairyō*	improvement, reform	321
改新	*kaishin*	renovation, reformation	174
改名	*kaimei*	changing one's name	82

515	酉 一 丨 7e 1a2 1b	**HAI, kuba(ru)** – distribute, pass out

配

心配	shinpai	worry, concern	97
支配	shihai	management, administration, rule	318
配達	haitatsu	deliver	448
配置	haichi	arrangement, placement	426
気配	kehai	sign, indication	134

516	酉 攵 ヽ 7e 4i 2o	**SAN, su(i)** – acid, sour

酸

酸味	sanmi	acidity, sourness	307
酸性	sansei	acidity	98
酸化	sanka	oxidation	254
酸素	sanso	oxygen	271
青酸	seisan	prussic acid, hydrogen cyanide	208

517	氵 酉 3a 7e	**SHU, sake, [saka]** – saké, rice wine, liquor

酒

日本酒	nihonshu	saké Japanese rice wine	5, 25
ぶどう酒	budōshu	(grape) wine	
禁酒	kinshu	abstinence from drink; temperance	482
酒屋	sakaya	wine dealer, liquor store	167
酒場	sakaba	bar, saloon, tavern	154

518	宀 土 口 3m 3b 3d	**GAI** – injury, harm, damage

害

公害	kōgai	pollution	126
水害	suigai	flood damage, flooding	21
損害	songai	injury, loss	350
利害	rigai	advantages and disadvantages, interests	329
妨害	bōgai	hindrance, obstruction	513

519

519	リ 宀 土 2f 3m 3b				

KATSU, wa(ru) – divide, separate, split; **wa(reru)** – break, crack/split apart; **wari** – proportion; profit; 10 percent; **sa(ku)** – cut up; separate; spare (time)

分割	bunkatsu	division, partitioning	38
割合	wariai	rate, proportion, percentage	159
割引き	waribiki	discount	216

520

520	ノ 心 1c 4k

HITSU, kanara(zu) – surely, (be) sure (to), without fail

必要	hitsuyō	necessary, requisite	419
必死	hisshi	certain death; desperation	85
必読	hitsudoku	required reading	244
必勝	hisshō	sure victory	509
必ずしも…ない	kanarazushimo ... nai	not necessarily	

521

521	宀 罒 心 3m 5g 4k

KEN – law

憲法	kenpō	constitution	123
改憲	kaiken	constitutional revision	514
憲政	kensei	constitutional government	483
立憲	rikken	constitutional	121
官憲	kanken	the (government) authorities	326

522

522	一 土 ｜ 1a3 3b 1b2

DOKU – poison

毒薬	dokuyaku	poison	359
有毒	yūdoku	poisonous	265
中毒	chūdoku	poisoning	28
毒草	dokusō	poisonous plant	249
気の毒	kinodoku	pitiable, regrettable, unfortunate	134

523

一	禾	艹
1a	4a	3k

JŌ, no(ru) – get in/on, ride, take (a train); be fooled; ***no(seru)*** – let ride, take aboard; deceive, trick, take in

乗用車	*jōyōsha*	passenger car	107, 133
乗車券	*jōshaken*	(passenger) ticket	133, 506
乗組員	*norikumiin*	(ship's) crew	418, 163
乗っ取る	*nottoru*	take over, commandeer, hijack	65

524

阝	艹	十
2d	3k	2k

YŪ – mail

郵便局	*yūbinkyoku*	post office	330, 170
郵便配達(人)	*yūbin haitatsu(nin)*	mailman	330, 515, 448, 1
郵便料金	*yūbin ryōkin*	postage	330, 319, 23
郵税	*yūzei*	postage	399
郵送料	*yūsōryō*	postage	441, 319

525

戈	一	丨
4n	1a	1b

SHIKI – ceremony, rite; style, form, method; formula

正式	*seishiki*	prescribed form, formal	275
公式	*kōshiki*	formula (in mathematics); formal, official	126
様式	*yōshiki*	mode, style	403
方式	*hōshiki*	formula, mode; method, system	70
新式	*shinshiki*	new type	174

526

言	戈	一
7a	4n	1a

SHI, kokoro(miru), tame(su) – give it a try, try out, attempt

試合	*shiai*	game, match	159
試作	*shisaku*	trial manufacture/cultivation	360
試食	*shishoku*	sample, taste	322
試運転	*shiunten*	trial run	439, 433
試金石	*shikinseki*	touchstone; test	23, 78

527	口 イ 一 3d4 2a 1a	**KI, *utsuwa*** – container, apparatus; capacity, ability

楽器	*gakki*	musical instrument	358
器楽	*kigaku*	instrumental music	358
器具	*kigu*	utensil, appliance, tool, apparatus	420
食器	*shokki*	eating utensils	322
不/無器用	*(bu)kiyō*	(not) dexterous	94, 93, 107

器　器　器

器　器　器

528	木 戈 イ 4a 4n 2a	***KI*** – opportunity; machine; ***hata*** – loom

機関	*kikan*	engine; machinery, organ, medium	398
制動機	*seidōki*	a brake	427, 231
起重機	*kijūki*	crane	373, 227
機能	*kinō*	a function	386
機会	*kikai*	opportunity, occasion, chance	158

機　機　機

機　機　機

529	木 戈 艹 4a 4n 3k	***KAI*** – fetters; machine

器械	*kikai*	instrument, apparatus, appliance	527
機械	*kikai*	machine, machinery	528
機械化	*kikaika*	mechanization	528, 254
機械文明	*kikai bunmei*	technological civilization	528, 111, 18

械　械　械

械　械　械

530	一 丨 ノ 1a2 1b 1c3	***HI, to(bu)*** – fly; ***to(basu)*** – let fly; skip over, omit

飛行	*hikō*	flight, aviation	68
飛行機	*hikōki*	airplane	68, 528
飛行場	*hikōjō*	airport	68, 154
飛び石	*tobiishi*	stepping-stones	78
飛び火	*tobihi*	flying sparks, leaping flames	20

飛　飛　飛

飛　飛　飛

531	木 口 亻 4a 3s 2a2	**KEN** – investigation, inspection		
		検事	*kenji*	public procurator/prosecutor	80
		検定	*kentei*	official approval, inspection	355
		検証	*kenshō*	verification, inspection	484
		検死	*kenshi*	coroner's inquest, autopsy	85
		点検	*tenken*	inspection, examination	169

検　検　検

検　検　検

532	馬 口 亻 10a 3s 2a2	**KEN** – effect; testing; [GEN] – beneficial effect		
		実験	*jikken*	experiment	203
		試験	*shiken*	examination, test	526
		入学試験	*nyūgaku shiken*	entrance exam	52, 109, 526
		体験	*taiken*	experience	61
		受験	*juken*	take a test/exam	260

験　験　験

験　験　験

533	阝 口 亻 2d 3s 2a2	**KEN, kewa(shii)** – steep, inaccessible; stern, harsh		
		保険	*hoken*	insurance	489
		険悪	*ken'aku*	dangerous, threatening	304
		険路	*kenro*	steep path	151
		険しい路	*kewashii michi*	steep/treacherous road	149
		険しい顔つき	*kewashii kaotsuki*	stern/fierce look	277

険　険　険

険　険　険

534	夕 厂 一 2n 2p 1a	**KI, abu(nai), aya(ui)** – dangerous		
		危険	*kiken*	danger	533
		危機	*kiki*	crisis, critical moment	528
		危急	*kikyū*	emergency, crisis	303
		危害	*kigai*	injury, harm	518
		危ぐ	*kigu*	fear, misgivings, apprehension	

危　危　危

危　危　危

535	扌 木 宀
	3c 4a 2i

TAN, sagu(ru) – search/grope for; **saga(su)** – look for

探検/険	*tanken*	exploration, expedition	531, 533
探知	*tanchi*	detection	214
探り出す	*saguridasu*	spy/sniff out (a secret)	53
探し回る	*sagashimawaru*	look/search around for	90

探 探 探

探 探 探

536	氵 木 宀
	3a 4a 2i

SHIN, fuka(i) – deep; **fuka(meru/maru)** – make/become deeper, more intense

深度	*shindo*	depth, deepness	377
深夜	*shin'ya*	dead of night, late at night	471
情け深い	*nasakebukai*	compassionate, merciful	209
興味深い	*kyōmibukai*	very interesting	368, 307

深 深 深

深 深 深

537	糸 氵 一
	6a 3a 1a3

RYOKU, [ROKU], midori – green

緑地	*ryokuchi*	green tract of land	118
新緑	*shinryoku*	fresh verdure/greenery	174
葉緑素	*yōryokuso*	chlorophyll	253, 271
緑青	*rokushō*	verdigris, green/copper rust	208
緑色	*midoriiro*	green, green-colored	204

緑 緑 緑

緑 緑 緑

538	金 氵 一
	8a 3a 1a3

ROKU – record

記録	*kiroku*	record	371
録音	*rokuon*	(sound) recording	347
録画	*rokuga*	videotape recording	274
目録	*mokuroku*	catalog, inventory, list	55
付録	*furoku*	supplement, appendix, addendum	192

録 録 録

録 録 録

539	一 ノ 1a2　1c	**YO, ata(eru)** – give, grant		

与党	yotō	party in power, government	495
関与	kan'yo	participation	398
給与	kyūyo	allowance, wage	346
供与	kyōyo	give, grant, furnish	197
賞与	shōyo	bonus	500

540	冖 一 ノ 2i　1a2　1c	**SHA, utsu(su)** – copy down; copy, duplicate; depict; photograph; *utsu(ru)* – be taken, turn out (photo)

写真	shashin	photograph	422
映写機	eishaki	projector	352, 528
写生	shasei	sketch, painting from nature	44
写実的	shajitsuteki	realistic, graphic	203, 210

541	十 土 一 (2k)　3b　1a	**KŌ, kanga(eru)** – think, consider

思考	shikō	thinking, thought	99
考案	kōan	conception, idea, design	106
考証	kōshō	historical research	484
考古学	kōkogaku	archaeology	172, 109
考え方	kangaekata	way of thinking, viewpoint	70

542	十 土 子 (2k)　3b　2c	**KŌ** – filial piety

(親)孝行	(oya)kōkō	filial piety, obedience to parents	175, 68
孝養	kōyō	discharge of filial duties	402
(親)不孝	(oya)fukō	undutifulness to one's parents	175, 94

543

十 土 卜
(2k) 3b 2m

RŌ, o(iru), fu(keru) – grow old

老人	*rōjin*	old man/woman/people	1
長老	*chōrō*	elder, senior member	95
元老	*genrō*	genro; elder statesman	137
老夫婦	*rōfūfu*	old married couple	315, 316
老子	*Rōshi*	Laozi, Lao-tzu	103

老　老　老

老 老 老

544

艹 口 厂
3k 3d 2p

JAKU, [NYAKU], waka(i) – young; **mo(shikuwa)** – or

老若	*rōnyaku, rōjaku*	young and old, youth and age	543
若者	*wakamono*	young man/people	164
若手	*wakate*	young man, younger member	57
若人	*wakōdo*	young man, a youth	1
若死に	*wakajini*	die young	85

若　若　若

若 若 若

545

艹 口 十
3k 3d 2k

KU, kuru(shimu) – suffer; **kuru(shimeru)** – torment; **kuru(shii)** – painful; **niga(i)** – bitter; **niga(ru)** – scowl

苦労	*kurō*	trouble, hardship, adversity	233
苦心	*kushin*	pains, efforts	97
病苦	*byōku*	the pain of illness	380
重苦しい	*omokurushii*	oppressed, gloomy, ponderous	227

苦　苦　苦

苦 苦 苦

546

車 月 亻
7c 4b 2a

YU – send, transport

輸入	*yunyū*	import	52
輸出	*yushutsu*	export	53
輸送	*yusō*	transport	441
運輸	*un'yu*	transport, conveyance	439
空輸	*kūyu*	air transport, shipment by air	140

輸　輸　輸

輸 輸 輸

547	車 土 又 7c 3b 2h	**KEI, karu(i), karo(yaka)** – light	
		軽工業	keikōgyō	light industry	139, 279
		軽食	keishoku	light meal	322
		軽音楽	keiongaku	light music	347, 358
		気軽	kigaru	lighthearted, cheerful, feel free (to)	134
		手軽	tegaru	easy, light, simple, cheap	57

548	糸 土 又 6a 3b 2h	**KEI** – longitude; sutra; passage of time; **KYŌ** – sutra; **he(ru)** – pass, elapse	
		経験	keiken	experience	532
		経歴	keireki	one's life history, career	480
		経理	keiri	accounting	143
		神経	shinkei	a nerve	310

549	氵 宀 一 3a 2j 1a2	**SAI, su(mu)** – come to an end; be paid; suffice; **su(masu)** – finish, settle; pay; make do, manage	
		経済	keizai	economy, economics	548
		返済	hensai	payment, repayment	442
		決済	kessai	settlement of accounts	356
		使用済み	shiyōzumi	used up	331, 107

550	刂 宀 一 2f 2j 1a2	**ZAI** – medicine, dose	
		薬剤	yakuzai	medicine, drug	359
		薬剤師	yakuzaishi	pharmacist, druggist	359, 409
		調剤	chōzai	compounding/preparation of medicines	342
		下剤	gezai	laxative	31
		解毒剤	gedokuzai	antidote	474, 522

551

才 十 ノ
2k 1c

SAI – talent, genius

天才	tensai	a genius	141
才子	saishi	talented person	103
才能	sainō	talent, ability	386
多才	tasai	many-talented	229
十八才	jūhassai	18 years old	12, 10

552

材 木 十 ノ
4a 2k 1c

ZAI – wood; material; talent

材料	zairyō	materials, ingredients	319
取材	shuzai	collection of material, news gathering	65
教材	kyōzai	teaching materials	245
題材	daizai	subject matter, theme	354
材木	zaimoku	wood, lumber	22

553

財 貝 十 ノ
7b 2k 1c

ZAI, [SAI] – money, wealth, property

財産	zaisan	estate, assets, property	278
財政	zaisei	finances, financial affairs	483
財務	zaimu	financial affairs	235
財界	zaikai	financial world, business circles	454
文化財	bunkazai	cultural asset	111, 254

554

因 口 亻 一
3s 2a 1a

IN – cause; **yo(ru)** – depend (on); be limited (to)

原因	gen'in	cause	136
主因	shuin	primary/main cause	155
死因	shiin	cause of death	85
要因	yōin	important factor, chief cause	419
因果	inga	cause and effect	487

555

心 □ 亻
4k 3s 2a

恩

ON – kindness, goodness; favor; gratitude

恩給	*onkyū*	pension	346
恩賞	*onshō*	a reward	500
恩人	*onjin*	benefactor; patron	1
恩返し	*ongaeshi*	repayment of a favor	442
恩知らず	*onshirazu*	ingratitude; ingrate	214

556

氵 艹 □
3a 3k 3s

漢

KAN – Han (Chinese dynasty), China; man, fellow

漢字	*kanji*	Chinese character	110
漢文	*kanbun*	Chinese writing; Chinese classics	111
漢時代	*kanjidai*	Han dynasty/period	42, 256
好/悪漢	*kō/ak-kan*	nice fellow/scoundrel, villain	104, 304
門外漢	*mongaikan*	outsider, layman	161, 83

557

隹 艹 □
8c 3k 3s

難

NAN, muzuka(shii), kata(i) – difficult

難題	*nandai*	difficult problem/question	354
難病	*nanbyō*	incurable disease	380
難民	*nanmin*	refugees	177
海難	*kainan*	disaster at sea, shipwreck	117
非難	*hinan*	adverse criticism	498

558

□ 木
3s 4a

困

KON, koma(ru) – be distressed

困難	*konnan*	difficulty, trouble	557
困苦	*konku*	hardships, adversity	545
困り果てる	*komarihateru*	be greatly troubled, nonplussed	487
困り切る	*komarikiru*	be in a bad fix, at a loss	39

559	力 ⺾ 口 2g 3k 3s	**KIN, [GON], tsuto(meru)** – be employed; **tsuto(maru)** – be fit for

勤労	kinrō	work, labor	233
勤務	kinmu	service, being on duty/at work	235
通勤	tsūkin	going to work, commuting	150
転勤	tenkin	be transferred (to another job)	433

勤　勤　勤

勤　勤　勤

560	扌 厂 一 3c 2p 1a2	**TEI** – resist

| 抵当 | teitō | mortgage, hypothec | 77 |
| 大抵 | taitei | generally, for the most part, usually | 26 |

抵　抵　抵

抵　抵　抵

561	亻 厂 一 2a 2p 1a2	**TEI, hiku(i)** – low; **hiku(meru/maru)** – make/become lower

最低	saitei	lowest, minimum	263
低地	teichi	low ground, lowlands	118
低所得	teishotoku	low income	153, 374
低成長	teiseichō	low growth	261, 95
低能	teinō	weak intellect, mental deficiency	386

低　低　低

低　低　低

562	广 厂 一 3q 2p 1a2	**TEI, soko** – bottom

根底	kontei	base, foundation	314
海底	kaitei	bottom of the sea, ocean floor	117
河底	katei	bottom of a river, riverbed	389
底力	sokojikara	latent energy/power	100
底値	sokone	rock-bottom price	425

底　底　底

底　底　底

563	阝 厂 一 2d 2p 1a2	***TEI*** – mansion, residence

邸

公邸	*kōtei*	official residence	126
官邸	*kantei*	official residence	326
私邸	*shitei*	one's private residence	125
邸宅	*teitaku*	residence, mansion	178
邸内	*teinai*	the grounds, the premises	84

564	夂 木 4i 4a	***JŌ*** – article, clause; line, stripe

条

条約	*jōyaku*	treaty	211
条文	*jōbun*	the text, provisions	111
第一条	*daiichijō*	Article 1 (in a law/contract/treaty)	404, 2
条理	*jōri*	logic, reason	143
信条	*shinjō*	a belief, article of faith	157

565	刂 士 亻 2f 3b 2a	***KEI, chigi(ru)*** – pledge, vow, promise

契

| 契約 | *keiyaku* | contract | 211 |
| 契機 | *keiki* | opportunity, chance | 528 |

566	ノ 厂 、 (1c) 2p 1d	***SHI*** – family, surname; Mr.; ***uji*** – family, lineage

氏

氏名	*shimei*	(full) name	82
坂本氏	*Sakamoto-shi*	Mr. Sakamoto	443, 25
同氏	*dōshi*	the said person, he	198
両氏	*ryōshi*	both (gentlemen)	200
氏神	*ujigami*	tutelary deity, genius loci	310

567	女 日 厂 3e 4c 2p	**KON** – marriage			
婚		結婚	*kekkon*	marriage	485
		結婚式	*kekkonshiki*	marriage ceremony, wedding	485, 525
		婚約	*kon'yaku*	engagement	211
		未婚	*mikon*	unmarried	306
		新婚旅行	*shinkon ryokō*	honeymoon	174, 222, 68

568	糸 亻 一 6a 2a 1a	**KYŪ** – rank, class			
級		進級	*shinkyū*	(school/military) promotion	437
		高級	*kōkyū*	high rank; high class, de luxe	190
		上級	*jōkyū*	upper grade, senior	32
		学級	*gakkyū*	class in school	109
		同級生	*dōkyūsei*	classmate	198, 44

569	⺮ 土 十 6f 3b 2k	**TŌ** – class, grade; equality; etc.; ***hito(shii)*** – equal			
等		等級	*tōkyū*	class, grade, rank	568
		一等	*ittō*	first class	2
		平等	*byōdō*	equality	202
		同等	*dōtō*	equality, same rank	198
		高等学校	*kōtō gakkō*	senior high school	190, 109, 115

570	言 土 十 7a 3b 2k	**SHI** – poetry, poem			
詩		詩人	*shijin*	poet	1
		詩歌	*shiika, shika*	poetry	392
		詩情	*shijō*	poetic sentiment	209
		詩集	*shishū*	collection of poems	436
		漢詩	*kanshi*	Chinese poem/poetry	556

571	侍 士 十 2a 3b 2k	**JI, samurai** – samurai

侍者	*jisha*	attendant, valet, page	164
侍女	*jijo*	lady-in-waiting, lady's attendant	102
侍医	*jii*	court physician	220
侍気質	*samurai katagi*	the samurai spirit	134, 176
七人の侍	*Shichinin no Samurai*	(The Seven Samurai)	9, 1

572	士 3p	**SHI** – samurai, man, scholar

人間同士	*ningen dōshi*	fellow human being	1, 43, 198
力士	*rikishi*	sumo wrestler	100
代議士	*daigishi*	dietman, congressman, M.P.	256, 292
学士	*gakushi*	university graduate	109
税理士	*zeirishi*	(licensed) tax accountant	399, 143

573	士 心 3p 4k	**SHI, kokorozashi** – will, intention, aim; **kokoroza(su)** – intend, aim at, have in view

意志	*ishi*	will	132
志向	*shikō*	intention, inclination	199
同志	*dōshi*	like-minded (person)	198
有志	*yūshi*	voluntary; those interested	265

574	言 心 士 7a 4k 3p	**SHI** – write down, chronicle; magazine

誌上	*shijō*	in a magazine	32
誌面	*shimen*	page of a magazine	274
日誌	*nisshi*	diary	5
地誌	*chishi*	a topography, geographical description	118
書誌学	*shoshigaku*	bibliography	131, 109

575 雑 8c 4a 1a

ZATSU, ZŌ – miscellany, a mix

雑誌	zasshi	magazine	574
雑音	zatsuon	noise, static	347
雑感	zakkan	miscellaneous thoughts/impressions	262
雑草	zassō	weeds	249
雑木林	zōkibayashi	thicket of assorted trees	22, 127

576 殺 4a 2s 2h

SATSU, [SAI], [SETSU], koro(su) – kill

自殺	jisatsu	suicide	62
暗殺	ansatsu	assassination	348
毒殺	dokusatsu	killing by poison	522
殺人	satsujin	a murder	1
人殺し	hitogoroshi	murder, murderer	1

577 設 7a 2s 2h

SETSU, mō(keru) – establish, set up, prepare

設立	setsuritsu	establishment, founding	121
設置	setchi	establishment, founding, institution	426
設定	settei	establishment, creation	355
新設	shinsetsu	newly established/organized	174
私設	shisetsu	private	125

578 命 2a 3d 2e

MEI – command; fate; life; **MYŌ, inochi** – life

生命 (保険)	seimei (hoken)	life (insurance)	44, 489, 533
運命	unmei	fate	439
使命	shimei	mission, errand	331
短命	tanmei	a short life	215
任命	ninmei	appointment, nomination	334

579 念
イ 心 一
2a 4k 1a2

NEN – thought, idea; desire; concern, attention

記念日	kinenbi	memorial day, anniversary	371, 5
記念切手	kinen kitte	commemorative stamp	371, 39, 57
理念	rinen	idea, doctrine, ideology	143
信念	shinnen	belief, faith, conviction	157
念入り	nen'iri	careful, scrupulous, thorough	52

580 源
氵 日 丷
3a 4c 3n

GEN, minamoto – source, origin

起源	kigen	origin	373
根源	kongen	origin	314
財源	zaigen	source of revenue	553
源平	Gen-Pei	Genji and Heike clans	202
源氏物語	Genji Monogatari	(The Tale of Genji)	566, 79, 67

581 願
頁 日 丷
9a 4c 3n

GAN, nega(u) – petition, request, desire

大願	taigan	great ambition, earnest wish	26
念願	nengan	one's heart's desire	579
出願	shutsugan	application	53
願書	gansho	written request, application	131
志願	shigan	application, volunteering, desire	573

582 払
扌 ノ 丶
3c 1c 1d

FUTSU, hara(u) – pay; sweep away

払底	futtei	shortage, scarcity	562
支払い	shiharai	payment	318
前払い	maebarai	payment in advance	47
現金払い	genkinbarai	cash payment	298, 23
分割払い	bunkatsubarai	payment in installments	38, 519

583	イ ノ 丶 2a 1c 1d	**BUTSU, hotoke** – Buddha				
		仏教	bukkyō	Buddhism		245
		大仏	daibutsu	great statue of Buddha		26
		石仏	sekibutsu	stone image of Buddha		78
		念仏	nenbutsu	Buddhist prayer		579
		日仏	Nichi-Futsu	Japanese-French		5

仏 仏 仏

仏 仏 仏

584	十 一 2k 1a	**KAN, hi(ru)** – get dry; **ho(su)** – dry; drink up			
		(潮の)干満	(shio no) kanman	tide, ebb and flow	467, 201
		干潮	kanchō	ebb/low tide	467
		干渉	kanshō	interfere, meddle	432
		若干	jakkan	some, a number of	544
		物干し	monohoshi	frame for drying clothes	79

干 干 干

干 干 干

585	リ 十 一 2f 2k 1a	**KAN** – publish			
		週刊(誌)	shūkan(shi)	weekly magazine	92, 574
		日刊紙	nikkanshi	daily newspaper	5, 180
		夕刊	yūkan	evening newspaper/edition	81
		新刊	shinkan	new publication	174
		未刊行	mikankō	unpublished	306, 68

刊 刊 刊

刊 刊 刊

586	屮 厂 十 3o 2p 2k	**GAN, kishi** – bank, shore, coast			
		西岸	seigan	west bank/coast	72
		対岸	taigan	opposite shore	365
		海岸	kaigan	seashore, coast	117
		河岸	kawagishi, kagan	riverbank	389
		川岸	kawagishi	riverbank	33

岸 岸 岸

岸 岸 岸

587	日 ト ノ 4c 2m2 1c	**KAI, mina** – all			
		皆済	kaisai	payment in full	549
		皆勤	kaikin	perfect attendance (at work/school)	559
		皆さん	minasan	everybody; Ladies and Gentlemen!	
		皆目	kaimoku	utterly; (not) at all	55
		皆無	kaimu	nothing/none at all	93

皆

588	阝 日 ト 2d 4c 2m2	**KAI** – stair, story, level			
		三階	sangai, sankai	third floor	4
		階段	kaidan	stairs, stairway	362
		段階	dankai	stage, phase	362
		階級	kaikyū	social class	568
		音階	onkai	musical scale	347

階

589	阝 土 ト 2d 3b 2m2	**HEI** – steps (of the throne)			
		天皇陛下	tennō-heika	H.M. the Emperor	141, 297, 31
		国王陛下	kokuō-heika	H.M. the King	40, 294, 31
		女王陛下	joō-heika	H.M. the Queen	102, 294, 31
		両陛下	ryōheika	Their Majesties the Emperor and Empress	200, 31

陛

590	冫 一 2b2 1a2	**U, ha, hane** – feather, wing			
		羽毛	umō	feather, plumage	287
		白羽	shiraha	white feather	205
		羽音	haoto	flapping of wings	347
		一羽	ichiwa	1 bird	2
		羽田	Haneda	(airport in Tokyo)	35

羽

591

習
4c 2b2 1a2

SHŪ, nara(u) – learn

学習	gakushū	learning, study	109
独習	dokushū	self-study	219
予習	yoshū	preparation of lessons	393
常習	jōshū	custom; habit	497
習字	shūji	penmanship, calligraphy	110

592

翌
5b 2b2 1a2

YOKU – the next, following

翌朝	yokuasa, yokuchō	the next morning	469
翌日	yokujitsu	the next/following day	5
翌週	yokushū	the following week, the week after that	92
翌年	yokunen	the following year	45
翌々日	yokuyokujitsu	2 days later/thereafter	5

593

談
7a 4d2

DAN – conversation

会談	kaidan	a conversation, conference	158
対談	taidan	face-to-face talk, conversation	365
談話	danwa	conversation	238
相談	sōdan	consultation	146
下相談	shitasōdan	preliminary negotiations	31, 146

594

訳
7a 3r 1d

YAKU – translation; *wake* – reason; meaning; circumstances

通訳	tsūyaku	interpreting, interpreter	150
英訳	eiyaku	a translation into English	353
全訳	zen'yaku	a complete translation	89
訳者	yakusha	translator	164
言い訳	iiwake	apology; excuse	66

595	米 尸 、 6b 3r 1d	**SHAKU** – explanation			
		解釈	*kaishaku*	interpretation, construal	474
		釈明	*shakumei*	explanation, vindication	18
		釈放	*shakuhō*	release, discharge	512
		保釈	*hoshaku*	(prison) bail	489
		注釈	*chūshaku*	comments, annotation	357

釈

596	米 田 冫 6b 5f 2b2	**HON, hirugae(su)** – (tr.) turn over; change (one's opinion); wave (a flag); **hirugae(ru)** – (intr.) turn over; wave			
		翻訳	*hon'yaku*	translation, translate	594
		翻案	*hon'an*	an adaptation	106
		翻意	*hon'i*	change one's mind	132
		翻ろう	*honrō*	trifle with, make sport of	

翻

597	木 口 4a 3d2	**KYŌ, hashi** – bridge			
		歩道橋	*hodōkyō*	pedestrian bridge	431, 149
		鉄橋	*tekkyō*	iron bridge; railway bridge	312
		石橋	*ishibashi*	stone bridge	78
		つり橋	*tsuribashi*	suspension bridge	
		日本橋	*Nihonbashi*	(area of Tokyo)	5, 25

橋

598	木 王 、 4a 4f 1d	**CHŪ, hashira** – pillar, column, pole			
		支柱	*shichū*	prop, support, strut	318
		電柱	*denchū*	utility/electric pole	108
		水銀柱	*suiginchū*	column of mercury	21, 313
		円柱	*enchū*	column, cylinder	13
		大黒柱	*daikokubashira*	central pillar, mainstay	26, 206

柱

599	馬 王 丶 10a 4f 1d	**CHŪ** – stop; reside	

駐車場　　*chūshajō*　　parking lot　　　　　　　　　　　133, 154
駐在　　　*chūzai*　　　stay, residence　　　　　　　　　　268
駐日　　　*chūnichi*　　resident/stationed in Japan　　　　5
進駐　　　*shinchū*　　stationing, occupation　　　　　　437

駐

駐 駐 駐

駐 駐 駐

600	一 日 十 (1a) 4c 2k2	**SEN, moppa(ra)** – entirely, exclusively	

専門家　　　*senmonka*　　　specialist, expert　　　　　　　161, 165
専任　　　　*sennin*　　　　exclusive duty, full-time　　　　334
専制　　　　*sensei*　　　　absolutism, despotism　　　　　427
専売　　　　*senbai*　　　　monopoly　　　　　　　　　　239
専用 (駐車場)　*sen'yō (chūshajō)*　private (parking lot)　107, 599, 133, 154

専

専 専 専

専 専 専

601	十 日 丶 2k3 4c 1d2	**HAKU, [BAKU]** – extensive, broad, many	

博物館　　*hakubutsukan*　museum　　　　　　　　　　79, 327
博学　　　*hakugaku*　　broad knowledge, erudition　　　109
博士　　　*hakase, hakushi*　doctor　　　　　　　　　　572
博愛　　　*hakuai*　　　philanthropy　　　　　　　　　259
万博　　　*banpaku*　　international exhibition　　　　　16

博

博 博 博

博 博 博

602	扌 ⺍ 一 3c 3n 2i	**JU, sazu(keru)** – grant, teach; **sazu(karu)** – be granted, taught	

授業　　　*jugyō*　　teaching, instruction　　　　　　279
教授　　　*kyōju*　　instruction; professor　　　　　245
授受　　　*juju*　　　giving and receiving, transfer　　260
授与　　　*juyo*　　　conferment, presentation　　　　539
授賞　　　*jushō*　　receiving a prize　　　　　　　500

授

授 授 授

授 授 授

603	石 隹 宀 5a 8c 2i	**KAKU**, *tashi(ka)* – certain; *tashi(kameru)* – make sure of, verify

確立	kakuritsu	establishment, settlement	121
確定	kakutei	decision, settlement	355
確実	kakujitsu	certain, reliable	203
確信	kakushin	firm belief, conviction	157
正確	seikaku	accurate, precise, correct	275

604	目 隹 ⺌ 5c 8c 2o	**KAN** – appearance, view

観光	kankō	sight-seeing, tourism	138
外観	gaikan	(external) appearance	83
主観的	shukanteki	subjective	155, 210
楽観的	rakkanteki	optimistic	358, 210
観念	kannen	idea; sense (of duty/justice)	579

605	⺌ 目 宀 3n 5c 2i	**KAKU**, *obo(eru)* – remember, bear in mind, learn; feel; *sa(meru/masu)* – (intr./tr.) awake, wake up

感覚	kankaku	sense, sensation, feeling	262
直覚	chokkaku	intuition, insight	423
見覚え	mioboe	recognition, knowing by sight	63
目覚まし (時計)	mezamashi(-dokei)	alarm clock	55, 42, 340

606	ネ 目 ⺀ 4e 5c 2o	**SHI** – seeing, regarding as

視力	shiryoku	visual acuity, eyesight	100
近視	kinshi	nearsightedness, shortsightedness	445
重視	jūshi	attach importance to, stress	227
無視	mushi	ignore, disregard	93
視界	shikai	field of vision	454

607	目 イ ⺍ 5c 2a 2o	**KI** – standard, measure

規定	kitei	stipulations, provisions, regulations	355
定規	jōgi	ruler, square; standard, norm	355
正規	seiki	regular, formal, regulation	275
新規	shinki	new	174
法規	hōki	laws and regulations, legislation	123

規

規　規　規

規 規 規

608	貝 刂 7b 2f	**SOKU** – rule, law

規則	kisoku	rule, regulation	607
原則	gensoku	general rule, principle	136
法則	hōsoku	a law	123
変則	hensoku	irregularity, anomaly	257
会則	kaisoku	rules of an association	158

則

則　則　則

則 則 則

609	イ 貝 刂 2a 7b 2f	**SOKU, kawa** – side

側面	sokumen	side, flank	274
側近者	sokkinsha	one's close associates	445, 164
左側	hidarigawa	left side	75
反対側	hantaigawa	opposite side	324, 365
日本側	Nippongawa, Nihongawa	the Japanese side	5, 25

側

側　側　側

側 側 側

610	氵 貝 刂 3a 7b 2f	**SOKU, haka(ru)** – measure

測量	sokuryō	measurement, surveying	411
測定	sokutei	measuring	355
観測	kansoku	observation	604
目測	mokusoku	measurement by eye, estimation	55
予測	yosoku	estimate, forecast	393

測

測　測　測

測 測 測

611	刂 ケ 一 2f 2n 1a	**RETSU** – row			
		列車	*ressha*	train	133
		列島	*rettō*	chain of islands, archipelago	286
		列国	*rekkoku*	world powers, nations	40
		行列	*gyōretsu*	queue; procession; matrix	68
		後列	*kōretsu*	back row	48

列

612	亻 ケ 刂 2a 2n 2f	**REI** – example; custom, precedent; *tato(eru)* – compare			
		例外	*reigai*	exception	83
		特例	*tokurei*	special case, exception	282
		先例	*senrei*	previous example, precedent	50
		例年	*reinen*	normal year; every year	45
		条例	*jōrei*	regulations, ordinance	564

例

613	宀 丷 一 3m 2o 1a2	**KAN** – completion			
		完結	*kanketsu*	completion	485
		完全	*kanzen*	complete, perfect	89
		完成	*kansei*	completion, accomplishment	261
		未完成	*mikansei*	incomplete, unfinished	306, 261
		完敗	*kanpai*	complete defeat	511

完

614	阝 宀 丷 2d 3m 2o	**IN** – institution			
		病院	*byōin*	hospital	380
		入院	*nyūin*	admission to a hospital	52
		大学院	*daigakuin*	graduate school	26, 109
		養老院	*yōrōin*	old folks' home	402, 543
		両院	*ryōin*	both houses (of the Diet/Congress/Parliament)	200

院

615	ネ 4e	**JI, SHI, shime(su)** – show		
		公示	kōji	public announcement	126
		明示	meiji	clear statement	18
		教示	kyōji	instruction, teaching	245
		暗示	anji	hint, suggestion	348
		示談	jidan	out-of-court settlement	593

示　示　示　示

示　示　示

616	宀 ネ 3m 4e	**SHŪ, SŌ** – religion, sect		
		宗教	shūkyō	religion	245
		宗門	shūmon	sect	161
		宗徒	shūto	adherent, believer	430
		改宗	kaishū	conversion, become a convert	514
		宗家	sōke	the head family	165

宗　宗　宗

宗　宗　宗

617	ネ 夕 又 4e 2n 2h	**SAI, matsu(ru)** – deify, worship; **matsu(ri)** – festival		
		祭日	saijitsu	holiday; festival day	5
		百年祭	hyakunensai	centennial	14, 45
		文化祭	bunkasai	cultural festival	111, 254
		秋祭り	akimatsuri	autumn festival	462
		後の祭り	ato no matsuri	Too late!	48

祭　祭　祭

祭　祭　祭

618	阝 ネ 夕 2d 4e 2n	**SAI** – time, occasion; **kiwa** – side, brink, edge		
		国際	kokusai	international	40
		交際	kōsai	association, company, acquaintance	114
		実際	jissai	truth, reality, actual practice	203
		水際	mizugiwa	water's edge, shore	21
		際立つ	kiwadatsu	be conspicuous, stand out	121

際　際　際

際　際　際

619

宀 礻 夂
3m 4e 2n

察

SATSU – surmise, judge, understand, sympathize

観 察	*kansatsu*	observation	604
検 察	*kensatsu*	criminal investigation, prosecution	531
視 察	*shisatsu*	inspection, observation	606
考 察	*kōsatsu*	consideration, examination	541
明 察	*meisatsu*	discernment, keen insight	18

620

礻 丨
4e 1b

礼

REI, RAI – courtesy; salutation; gratitude, remuneration

祭 礼	*sairei*	religious festival	617
礼 式	*reishiki*	etiquette	525
失 礼	*shitsurei*	rudeness	311
非 礼	*hirei*	impoliteness	498
無 礼	*burei*	rudeness, impertinence, affront	93

621

礻 厂 一
4e 2p 1a

祈

KI, ino(ru) – pray

祈 念	*kinen*	a prayer	579
祈 願	*kigan*	a prayer	581
祈 とう (書)	*kitō(sho)*	prayer (book)	131
祈 り	*inori*	a prayer	
主 の 祈 り	*shu no inori*	the Lord's Prayer	155

622

礻 冂 一
4e 2r 1a3

祖

SO – ancestor

祖 先	*sosen*	ancestor, forefather	50
祖 母/父	*sobo/fu*	grandmother/father	112, 113
祖 国	*sokoku*	one's homeland/fatherland	40
元 祖	*ganso*	originator, founder, inventor	137
宗 祖	*shūso*	founder of a sect	616

623	力 冂 一 2g 2r 1a2	**JO, tasu(keru)** – help, rescue; **tasu(karu)** – be helped, rescued; **suke** – assistance	
助		助力　　　joryoku　　　help, assistance 助言　　　jogen　　　　advice 助手　　　joshu　　　　helper, assistant 助け合う　tasukeau　　　help each other	100 66 57 159

624	木 冂 一 4a 2r 1a3	**SA** – investigate	
査		調査　　　chōsa　　　　investigation, inquiry, observation 検査　　　kensa　　　　inspection, examination 査問　　　samon　　　　inquiry, hearing 査察　　　sasatsu　　　inspection, observation 査定　　　satei　　　　assessment	342 531 162 619 355

625	宀 日 一 3m 4c 1a2	**SEN** – announce	
宣		宣言　　　　sengen　　　　declaration, manifesto 独立宣言　dokuritsu sengen　declaration of independence 宣伝　　　　senden　　　　propaganda; advertising, publicity 宣戦　　　　sensen　　　　declaration of war 宣教師　　senkyōshi　　a missionary	66 219, 121, 66 434 301 245, 409

626	冫 犭 丨 2b 3g 1b	**JŌ** – condition, circumstances; form; letter	
状		状態　　　jōtai　　　　circumstances, situation 現状　　　genjō　　　present situation 白状　　　hakujō　　　confession 礼状　　　reijō　　　letter of thanks 招待状　　shōtaijō　　written invitation	387 298 205 620 455, 452

627

氵 丷 寸
2b 3n 2k

SHŌ – commander, general; soon

将来	shōrai	future	69
将軍	shōgun	shogun, general	438
大将	taishō	general, leader	26
主将	shushō	(team) captain	155
将校	shōkō	officer	115

将　将　将

将　将　将

628

扌 日 卜
3c 4c 2m

TEI – present, submit; **sa(geru)** – carry (in the hand)

提案	teian	proposition, proposal	106
提供	teikyō	offer	197
提議	teigi	proposal, suggestion	292
提出	teishutsu	presentation, filing	53
前提	zentei	premise	47

提　提　提

提　提　提

629

一 亻 、
1a 2a 1d

TAI, TA, futo(i) – fat, thick; **futo(ru)** – get fat/thick

太平洋	Taiheiyō	Pacific Ocean	202, 289
皇太子	kōtaishi	crown prince	297, 103
太古	taiko	ancient times, antiquity	172
太字	futoji	thick character, boldface	110
太刀	tachi	(long) sword	37

太　太　太

太　太　太

630

阝 日 一
2d 4c 1a2

YŌ – positive, male; sun

太陽	taiyō	sun	629
陽光	yōkō	sunshine, sunlight	138
陽気	yōki	season, weather; cheerfulness, gaiety	134
陽性	yōsei	positive	98
陽子	yōshi	proton	103

陽　陽　陽

陽　陽　陽

631 揚 扌3c 日4c 一1a2

YŌ, a(geru) – raise; fry; **a(garu)** – rise

高揚	kōyō	uplift, surge	190
揚水車	yōsuisha	scoop wheel	21, 133
意気揚々	ikiyōyō	triumphantly, exultantly	132, 134
荷揚げ	niage	unloading, discharge, landing	391
引き揚げ	hikiage	withdrawal, evacuation	216

632 湯 氵3a 日4c 一1a2

TŌ, yu – hot water

湯治	tōji	hot-spring cure	493
湯元	yumoto	source of a hot spring	137
湯ぶね	yubune	bathtub	
茶の湯	cha no yu	tea ceremony	251
湯上がり	yuagari	just after a bath	32

633 傷 亻2a 日4c 一1a3

SHŌ, kizu – wound, injury; **ita(mu)** – hurt; **ita(meru)** – injure

負傷	fushō	wound, injury	510
傷害	shōgai	injury, damage	518
重/軽傷	jū/keishō	severe/minor injuries	227, 547
死傷者	shishōsha	the killed and injured, casualties	85, 164
中傷	chūshō	slander	28

634 温 氵3a 皿5h 日4c

ON, atata(kai/ka) – warm; **atata(maru/meru)** – (intr./tr.) warm up

温度	ondo	temperature	377
気/水/体温	ki/sui/tai-on	air/water/body temperature	134, 21, 61
温室	onshitsu	hothouse, greenhouse	166
温和	onwa	mild, gentle	124

635

日 ⹀ 厂
4c 3n 2p

DAN, atata(kai/ka) – warm; **atata(maru/meru)** – (intr./tr.) warm up

寒暖計	kandankei	thermometer	457, 340
温暖	ondan	warm	634
暖流	danryū	warm ocean current	247
暖冬	dantō	warm/mild winter	459

636

雨 一 ノ
8d 1a2 1c

UN, kumo – cloud

風雲	fūun	wind and clouds; situation	29
暗雲	an'un	dark clouds	348
雨雲	amagumo	rain cloud	30
入道雲	nyūdōgumo	cumulonimbus, thunderhead	52, 149
出雲大社	Izumo Taisha	Izumo Shrine	53, 26, 308

637

日 雨 一
4c 8d 1a2

DON, kumo(ru) – cloud up, get cloudy

曇天	donten	cloudy/overcast sky	141
花曇り	hanagumori	cloudy weather in cherryblossom season	255
雲りがち	kumorigachi	broken clouds, mostly cloudy	
曇りガラス	kumorigarasu	ground/frosted/mat glass	

638

日 土 ノ
4c2 3b 1c

SHO, atsu(i) – hot (weather)

寒暑	kansho	cold and heat	457
暑気	shoki	the heat	134
暑中	shochū	middle of summer	28
大暑	taisho	Japanese Midsummer Day (about July 24)	26
暑苦しい	atsukurushii	oppressively hot, sultry	545

639	厂 日 子 2p 4c 2c	**KŌ, atsu(i)** – thick; kind, cordial		

厚意	kōi	kind intentions, kindness	132	
厚顔	kōgan	impudence, effrontery	277	
厚生省	Kōseishō	Ministry of Health and Welfare	44, 145	
厚相	kōshō	minister of health and welfare	146	
厚紙	atsugami	thick paper, cardboard	180	

640	宀 日 女 3m 4c 3e	**EN** – feast, banquet		

宴会	enkai	dinner party, banquet	158	
宴席	enseki	(one's seat in) a banquet hall	379	
酒宴	shuen	feast, drinking bout	517	
きょう宴	kyōen	banquet, feast, dinner		

641	宀 女 口 3m 4i 3d	**KYAKU, KAKU** – guest, customer		

客間/室	kyaku-ma/shitsu	guest room	43, 166	
客船	kyakusen	passenger ship	376	
乗客	jōkyaku	passenger	523	
旅客	ryokaku	passenger, traveler	222	
客観的	kyakkanteki	objective	604, 210	

642	女 口 4i 3d	**KAKU, onoono** – each, every; various		

各地	kakuchi	every area; various places	118	
各国	kakkoku	all/various countries	40	
各種	kakushu	every kind, various types	228	
各人	kakujin	each person, everyone	1	
各自	kakuji	each person, everyone	62	

643

木 攵 口
4a 4i 3d

格

KAKU, [KŌ] – status, rank; standard, rule; case

人格	jinkaku	personality, character	1
性格	seikaku	character, personality	98
価格	kakaku	price; value	421
合格	gōkaku	pass (an exam)	159
格子	kōshi	lattice, bars, grating, grille	103

644

一 丨 丶
1a 1b 1d

丸

GAN, maru(i) – round; **maru(meru)** – make round, form into a ball; **-maru** – (suffix for names of ships)

丸薬	gan'yaku	pill	359
丸太小屋	marutagoya	log cabin	629, 27, 167
日本丸	Nihonmaru	the ship Nihon	5, 25
日の丸	Hi no Maru	(Japanese) Rising-Sun Flag	5

645

火 土 ⺌
4d 3b2 2o

熱

NETSU – heat, fever; **atsu(i)** – hot (food)

熱病	netsubyō	fever	380
高熱	kōnetsu	high fever	190
熱湯	nettō	boiling water	632
情熱	jōnetsu	passion	209
熱心	nesshin	enthusiasm, zeal	97

646

力 土 ⺌
2g 3b2 2o

勢

SEI, ikio(i) – force, energy, vigor; trend

勢力	seiryoku	influence, force	100
国勢	kokusei	state/condition of a country	40
情勢	jōsei	the situation	209
大勢	taisei	general situation/trend	26
	ōzei	many people, large crowd	

647 陸

RIKU – land

大 陸	tairiku	continent, mainland	26
陸 上	rikujō	land, ground	32
上 陸	jōriku	landing, going ashore	32
陸 路	rikuro	land route	151
陸 軍	rikugun	army	438

648 銭

SEN – money; 1/100 yen; zeni – money

金 銭	kinsen	money	23
口 銭	kōsen	commission, percentage	54
悪 銭	akusen	ill-gotten money	304
銭 湯	sentō	public bath	632
小 銭	kozeni	small change	27

649 浅

SEN, asa(i) – shallow

浅 海	senkai	shallow sea	117
浅 見	senken	superficial view	63
浅 学	sengaku	superficial knowledge	109
浅 黒 い	asaguroi	dark-colored, swarthy	206
遠 浅	tōasa	shoaling beach	446

650 残

ZAN, noko(su/ru) – leave/remain behind

残 念	zannen	regret, disappointment, too bad	579
残 業	zangyō	overtime	279
残 高	zandaka	balance, remainder	190
残 り 物	nokorimono	leftovers	79
生 き 残 る	ikinokoru	survive	44

651	火 犭 ⺍ 4d 3g 2n	**ZEN, NEN** – as, like			
		全然	*zenzen*	(not) at all; completely	89
		当然	*tōzen*	naturally, (as a matter) of course	77
		必然	*hitsuzen*	inevitability, necessity	520
		自然	*shizen*	nature	62
		天然	*tennen*	natural	141

652	火 犭 ⺍ 4d2 3g 2n	**NEN, mo(eru)** – (intr.) burn; **mo(yasu/su)** – (tr.) burn			
		燃料	*nenryō*	fuel	319
		不燃性	*funensei*	nonflammable, fireproof	94, 98
		可燃性	*kanensei*	flammable, combustible	388, 98
		内燃機関	*nainen kikan*	internal-combustion engine	84, 528, 398
		燃え上がる	*moeagaru*	blaze up, burst into flames	32

653	⺍ 口 亻 2o 3d 2a	**KOKU, tani** – valley			
		谷間	*tanima*	valley	43
		谷底	*tanisoko*	bottom of a ravine/gorge	562
		谷川	*tanigawa*	mountain stream	33
		長谷川	*Hasegawa*	(surname)	95, 33
		四ツ谷	*Yotsuya*	(area of Tokyo)	6

654	宀 口 ⺍ 3m 3d 2o	**YŌ** – form, appearance; content			
		美容院	*biyōin*	beauty parlor, hairdresser's	401, 614
		形容	*keiyō*	form; metaphor	395
		内容	*naiyō*	content	84
		容器	*yōki*	container	527
		容量	*yōryō*	capacity, volume	411

655	貝 土 一 7b 3b 1a	**SEKI, se(meru)** – condemn, censure; torture

責任　　　*sekinin*　　　responsibility　　　　　　　　　334
重責　　　*jūseki*　　　 heavy responsibility　　　　 　227
責務　　　*sekimu*　　　duty, obligation　　　　　　　235
自責　　　*jiseki*　　　　self-reproach, pàngs of conscience　62
引責　　　*inseki*　　　 assume responsibility　　　　　216

656	禾 貝 土 5d 7b 3b	**SEKI, tsu(mu)** – heap up, load; **tsu(moru)** – be piled up, accumulate; **tsu(mori)** – intention; estimate

面積　　　　　*menseki*　　　(surface) area　　　　　　　　 274
積極的　　　　*sekkyokuteki*　 positive, active　　　　　 336, 210
積み重ねる　 *tsumikasaneru*　 stack up one on another　　　　227
見積 (書)　　 *mitsumori(sho)*　(written) estimate　　　　63, 131

657	` 目 王 2o 5c 4f	**CHAKU, [JAKU]** – arrival; clothing; **ki(ru), tsu(keru)** – put on, wear; **ki(seru)** – dress (someone); **tsu(ku)** – arrive

着陸　　　*chakuriku*　　 (airplane) landing　　　　　　 647
決着　　　*ketchaku*　　　conclusion, settlement, decision　356
着物　　　*kimono*　　　 kimono; clothing　　　　　　　79
下着　　　*shitagi*　　　　underwear　　　　　　　　　　31

658	` 王 一 2o 4f 1a2	**SA** – difference; **sa(su)** – hold (an umbrella); wear (a sword); offer (a cup of saké); thrust

時差　　　　*jisa*　　　　time difference/lag　　　　　　 42
差別　　　　*sabetsu*　　 discrimination　　　　　　　 267
交差点　　　*kōsaten*　　 intersection　　　　　　　114, 169
差し支え　 *sashitsukae*　impediment; objection　　　　 318

659	米 月 土
	6b 4b 3b

SEI, [SHŌ] – spirit; energy, vitality

精力	*seiryoku*	energy, vigor, vitality	100
精神	*seishin*	mind, spirit	310
精液	*seieki*	semen, sperm	472
精進	*shōjin*	diligence, devotion; purification	437
不/無精	*bushō*	sloth, laziness, indolence	94, 93

660	氵 月 土
	3a 4b 3b

SEI, [SHŌ], kiyo(i) – pure, clean, clear; **kiyo(meru)** – purify, cleanse; **kiyo(maru)** – be purified, cleansed

清酒	*seishu*	refined saké	517
清書	*seisho*	fair/clean copy	131
清水	*seisui, shimizu*	pure/clear water	21
	Kiyomizu	(temple in Kyoto)	

661	言 月 土
	7a 4b 3b

SEI, SHIN, ko(u) – ask for; **u(keru)** – receive

請願	*seigan*	petition, application	581
要請	*yōsei*	demand, requirement, request	419
申請	*shinsei*	application, petition	309
強請	*kyōsei*	importunate demand; extortion	217
下請け	*shitauke*	subcontract	31

662	日 月 土
	4c 4b 3b

SEI, ha(reru/rasu) – (intr./tr.) clear up

晴天	*seiten*	clear sky, fine weather	141
晴曇	*seidon*	changeable, fair to cloudy	637
秋晴れ	*akibare*	clear autumn weather	462
見晴らし	*miharashi*	view, vista	63
気晴らし	*kibarashi*	pastime, diversion	134

663

月 土 宀
4b 3b 2n

SEI, [JŌ], shizu, shizu(ka) – quiet, peaceful, still; *shizu(meru/maru)* – make/become peaceful

静 物	*seibutsu*	still life	79
静 止	*seishi*	stillness, rest, stationary	477
安 静	*ansei*	rest, quiet, repose	105
平 静	*heisei*	calm, serenity	202

664

氵 ⺈ 十
3a 2n 2k

JŌ – pure

清 浄	*seijō*	purity, cleanliness	660
浄 化	*jōka*	purification	254
不 浄	*fujō*	dirtiness, impurity	94
浄 土 宗	*Jōdoshū*	the Jodo sect (of Buddhism)	24, 616

665

石 厂 又
5a 2p 2h

HA, yabu(ru) – tear, break; *yabu(reru)* – get torn/broken

破 産	*hasan*	bankruptcy	278
破 局	*hakyoku*	catastrophe, ruin	170
破 約	*hayaku*	breach of contract/promise	211
破 れ 目	*yabureme*	a tear, split	55
見 破 る	*miyaburu*	see through	63

666

氵 厂 又
3a 2p 2h

HA, nami – wave

波 止 場	*hatoba*	wharf, pier	477, 154
電 波	*denpa*	electric/radio wave	108
短 波	*tanpa*	shortwave	215
波 長	*hachō*	wavelength	95
波 乗 り	*naminori*	surfing	523

667	彳 3i	十 2k	一 1a4	**RITSU, [RICHI]** – law, regulation	
				法律 *hōritsu*	law	123
				規律 *kiritsu*	order, discipline, regulations	607
				不文律 *fubunritsu*	unwritten law	94, 111
				韻律 *inritsu*	rhythm, meter	349
				自律神経 *jiritsu shinkei*	autonomic nerve	62, 310, 548

律

668	氵 3a	十 2k	一 1a4	**SHIN, tsu** – harbor, ferry
				津波 *tsunami* tsunami, "tidal" wave	666
				興味津々 *kyōmi-shinshin* very interesting	368, 307
				津軽半島 *Tsugaru Hantō* Tsugaru Peninsula	547, 88, 286

津

669	氵 3a	艹 3k	2o	**KŌ, minato** – harbor, port
				空港 *kūkō* airport	140
				商/軍港 *shō/gunkō* trading/naval port	412, 438
				内港 *naikō* inner harbor	84
				港内 *kōnai* in the harbor	84
				港町 *minatomachi* port city	182

港

670	氵 3a	弓 3h	亠 2j	**WAN** – bay
				東京湾 *Tōkyō-wan* Tokyo Bay	71, 189
				湾曲 *wankyoku* curvature, bend	366
				港湾 *kōwan* harbor	669
				港湾労働者 *kōwan rōdōsha* port laborer, longshoreman	669, 233, 232, 164
				台湾 *Taiwan* Taiwan	492

湾

671	女 十 一 3e 2k 1a3	**SAI, tsuma** – wife			
		夫 妻	*fusai*	husband and wife, Mr. and Mrs.	315
		妻 子	*saishi*	wife and child/children, family	103
		後 妻	*gosai*	second wife	48
		良 妻	*ryōsai*	good wife	321
		老 妻	*rōsai*	one's aged wife	543

672	亠 丨 2j 1b	**BŌ, [MŌ]** – die; **na(i)** – dead, deceased			
		死 亡 者	*shibōsha*	the dead	85, 164
		亡 父	*bōfu*	one's late father	113
		亡 夫	*bōfu*	one's late husband	315
		未 亡 人	*mibōjin*	widow	306, 1
		亡 命	*bōmei*	fleeing one's country, going into exile	578

673	王 月 亠 4f 4b 2j	**BŌ, MŌ, nozo(mu)** – desire, wish, hope for			
		志 望	*shibō*	wish, aspiration	573
		宿 望	*shukubō*	long-cherished desire	179
		要 望	*yōbō*	demand, wish	419
		失 望	*shitsubō*	despair, disappointment	311
		大 望	*taibō*	great desire, ambition	26

674	王 耳 口 4f 6e 3d	**SEI** – holy			
		聖 人	*seijin*	sage, holy man	1
		神 聖	*shinsei*	sacredness, sanctity	310
		聖 書	*seisho*	the Bible	131
		聖 堂	*seidō*	Confucian temple; church	496
		聖 母	*seibo*	the Holy Mother, the Blessed Mary	112

675 巾 厂 3f 2p	*FU* – spread; cloth; *nuno* – a cloth		
	財布	*saifu*	purse, wallet	553
	毛布	*mōfu*	a blanket	287
	分布	*bunpu*	distribution, range	38
	配布	*haifu*	distribution, distributing widely	515
	公布	*kōfu*	official announcement, promulgation	126

布

676 巾 厂 ノ 3f 2p 1c	*KI* – hope, desire; rarity, scarcity		
	希望	*kibō*	wish, hope	673
	メーカー希望価格	*mēkā kibō kakaku*	manufacturer's suggested price, list price	673, 421, 643
	希少	*kishō*	scarce, rare	144
	希少価値	*kishō kachi*	scarcity value	144, 421, 425

希

677 衤 5e	*I, koromo* – garment, clothes		
	衣類	*irui*	clothing	226
	黒衣	*kokui*	black clothes	206
	法衣	*hōi*	priestly robes, vestment	123
	衣食住	*ishokujū*	food, clothing, and shelter	322, 156
	羽衣	*hagoromo*	robe of feathers	590

衣

678 イ 衤 2a 5e	*I, [E]* – depend on, be due to; request		
	依存(度)	*izon(do)*	(extent of) dependence	269, 377
	依然として	*izen toshite*	as ever, as before	651
	帰依	*kie*	faith, devotion; conversion	317

依

679	ネ 刂 5e　2f	**SHO**, *haji(me)* – beginning; *haji(mete)* – for the first time; *hatsu-, ui-* – first; *-so(meru)* – begin to

初

最 初	*saisho*	beginning, first	263
初 歩	*shoho*	rudiments, ABCs	431
初 演	*shoen*	first performance, premiere	344
初 恋	*hatsukoi*	one's first love	258

初　初　初

初　初　初

680	糸 立 日 6a　5b　4c	**SHOKU, SHIKI**, *o(ru)* – weave

織

織 機	*shokki*	loom	528
組 織	*soshiki*	organization, structure; tissue	418
織 物	*orimono*	cloth, fabric, textiles	79
毛 織 (物)	*keori(mono)*	woolen fabric	287, 79
羽 織	*haori*	haori, Japanese half-coat	590

織　織　織

織　織　織

681	言 立 日 7a　5b　4c	**SHIKI** – know, discriminate

識

意 識	*ishiki*	consciousness	132
知 識	*chishiki*	knowledge	214
常 識	*jōshiki*	common sense/knowledge	497
学 識	*gakushiki*	learning	109
識 別	*shikibetsu*	discrimination, recognition	267

識　識　識

識　識　識

682	糸 戸 艹 6a　4m　3k	**HEN**, *a(mu)* – knit, crochet; compile, edit

編

編 集	*henshū*	editing	436
短 編 小 説	*tanpen shōsetsu*	short novel, story	215, 27, 400
編 成	*hensei*	organizing, formation	261
編 み 物	*amimono*	knitting; knitted goods	79
手 編 み	*teami*	knitting by hand	57

編　編　編

編　編　編

683	月 卩 又
	4b 2e 2h

FUKU – clothes, dress; dose

衣服	ifuku	clothing	677
洋/和服	yō/wa-fuku	Western/Japanese clothing	289, 124
心服	shinpuku	admiration and devotion	97
着服	chakufuku	embezzlement, misappropriation	657
服役	fukueki	penal servitude; military service	375

684	土 立 十
	(3b) 5b 2k

KŌ, saiwa(i), shiawa(se), sachi – happiness, good fortune

| 幸運 | kōun | good fortune, luck | 439 |
| 不幸 | fukō | unhappiness, misfortune | 94 |

685	土 立 十
	(3b) 5b 2k

HŌ – news, report; remuneration; **muku(iru)** – reward, requite

天気予報	tenki yohō	weather forecast	141, 134, 393
報道機関	hōdō kikan	news media, the press	149, 528, 398
情報	jōhō	information	209
報知	hōchi	information, news, intelligence	214
電報	denpō	telegram	108

686	土 立 十
	(3b) 5b 2k

SHITSU, SHŪ, to(ru) – take, grasp; carry out, execute

執行	shikkō	execution, performance	68
執権	shikken	regent	335
執心	shūshin	devotion, attachment, infatuation	97
執着	shūjaku, shūchaku	attachment to; tenacity	657
執念	shūnen	tenacity of purpose; vindictiveness	579

687	火 口 亠
	4d 3d 2j

JUKU, u(reru) – ripen, come to maturity

円熟	enjuku	maturity, mellowness	13
成熟	seijuku	ripeness, maturity	261
未熟	mijuku	unripe, immature, green	306
半熟	hanjuku	half-cooked, soft-boiled (egg)	88
熟語	jukugo	compound word; phrase	67

688	立 口 十
	5b 3b 2k2

JI – word; resignation; **ya(meru)** – quit, resign

辞書/典	jisho/ten	dictionary	131, 367
(お)世辞	(o)seji	compliment, flattery	252
式辞	shikiji	address, oration	525
辞職	jishoku	resignation	385
辞表	jihyō	(letter of) resignation	272

689	口 十 丨
	3d 2k 1b

RAN – riot, rebellion; disorder; **mida(su/reru)** – put/get in disorder, confusion

反乱	hanran	rebellion, insurgency, insurrection	324
内乱	nairan	internal strife, civil war	84
乱雑	ranzatsu	disorder, confusion	575
乱筆	ranpitsu	hasty writing, scrawl	130

690	口 土 ノ
	3d 3b 1c

KOKU, tsu(geru) – tell, announce, inform

報告	hōkoku	report	685
通告	tsūkoku	notice, notification	150
申告	shinkoku	report, declaration, (tax) return	309
告発	kokuhatsu	prosecution, indictment, accusation	96
告白	kokuhaku	confession, avowal, profession	205

691	辶 土 口			
	2q 3b 3d			

ZŌ, tsuku(ru) – produce, build

製造	seizō	manufacture, production	428
造船	zōsen	shipbuilding	376
木造	mokuzō	made of wood, wooden	22
人造	jinzō	man-made, artificial	1
手造り	tezukuri	handmade	57

692	氵 土 丷			
	3a 3b 2o			

SEN, ara(u) – wash

洗剤	senzai	detergent	550
洗面器	senmenki	wash basin	274, 527
洗面所	senmenjo	washroom, lavatory	274, 153
(お)手洗い	(o)tearai	washroom, lavatory	57
洗い立てる	araitateru	inquire into, rake up, ferret out	121

693	氵 一 ノ			
	3a 1a2 1c			

O, kitana(i), kega(rawashii) – dirty; **yogo(reru/su), kega(reru/su)** – become/make dirty

汚職	oshoku	corruption, bribery	385
汚物	obutsu	dirt, filth; sewage	79
汚点	oten	blot, blotch, blemish, tarnish	169
汚名	omei	stigma, stain on one's name, dishonor	82

694	广 ノ 丶			
	3q 1c 1d			

KŌ, hiro(i) – broad, wide; **hiro(geru)** – extend, enlarge; **hiro(garu)** – spread, expand; **hiro(meru)** – broaden, propagate; **hiro(maru)** – spread, be propagated

広告	kōkoku	advertisement	690
広大	kōdai	vast, extensive, huge	26
広場	hiroba	plaza, public square	154

695 糸 田
6a 5f

SAI – narrow, small, fine; **hoso(i)** – thin, narrow, slender; **hoso(ru)** – get thinner; **koma(kai/ka)** – small, detailed

委細	*isai*	details, particulars	466
細工	*saiku*	work, workmanship; artifice, trick	139
細説	*saisetsu*	detailed explanation	400
細長い	*hosonagai*	long and thin, lean and lanky	95

細　細　細

細　細　細

696 木 ゛ ノ
4a 2o 1c

SHŌ, matsu – pine

松原	*matsubara*	pine grove	136
松林	*matsubayashi*	pine woods	127
松葉	*matsuba*	pine needle	253
門松	*kadomatsu*	pine decoration for New Year's	161
松島	*Matsushima*	(scenic coastal area near Sendai)	286

松　松　松

松　松　松

697 糸 心 ゛
6a 4k 2o

SŌ – general, overall

総会	*sōkai*	general meeting, plenary session	158
総合	*sōgō*	synthesis, comprehensive	159
総計	*sōkei*	(sum) total	340
総理	*sōri*	prime minister (cf. No. 835)	143
国民総生産	*kokumin sōseisan*	gross national product	40, 177, 44, 278

総　総　総

総　総　総

698 宀 心 ゛
3m 4k 2o

SŌ, mado – window

同窓生	*dōsōsei*	schoolmate, alumnus	198, 44
車窓	*shasō*	car window	133
窓口	*madoguchi*	(ticket) window	54
二重窓	*nijūmado*	double window	3, 227
窓際の席	*madogiwa no seki*	seat next to the window	618, 379

窓　窓　窓

窓　窓　窓

699	氵 魚 3a 11a	**GYO, RYŌ** – fishing

漁業　　gyogyō　　fishery, fishing industry　　279
漁船　　gyosen　　fishing boat/vessel　　376
漁場　　gyojō　　fishing ground/banks　　154
漁村　　gyoson　　fishing village　　191
漁師　　ryōshi　　fisherman　　409

700	魚 口 ⼍ 11a 3d 3n	**GEI, kujira** – whale

白鯨　　Hakugei　　(Moby Dick, or The White Whale—Melville)　　205
鯨肉　　geiniku　　whale meat　　223
鯨油　　geiyu　　whale oil　　364
鯨飲　　geiin　　drink like a fish, guzzle　　323

701	魚 王 ⼍ 11a 4f 2o	**SEN, aza(yaka)** – fresh, vivid, clear, brilliant

新鮮　　shinsen　　fresh　　174
鮮明　　senmei　　clear, distinct　　18
鮮度　　sendo　　(degree of) freshness　　377
鮮魚　　sengyo　　fresh fish　　290
朝鮮　　Chōsen　　Korea　　469

702	辶 王 尸 2q 4f 3r	**CHI, oso(i)** – late, tardy; slow; **oku(reru)** – be late (for); be slow (clock); **oku(rasu)** – defer, put back (a clock)

遅着　　chichaku　　late arrival　　657
遅配　　chihai　　delay in apportioning/delivery　　515
遅速　　chisoku　　speed　　502
乗り遅れる　noriokureru　be too late to catch, miss (a bus)　　523

703

目 ˇ 辶
5c 2o 2q

DŌ, michibi(ku) – lead, guide

主導	shudō	leadership, guidance	155
先導	sendō	guidance, leadership	50
導入	dōnyū	introduction	52
導火線	dōkasen	fuse; cause, occasion	20, 299
半導体	handōtai	semiconductor	88, 61

704

ˇ 酉 十
2o 7e 2k

SON, tatto(bu), tōto(bu) – value, esteem, respect; **tatto(i), tōto(i)** – valuable, precious, noble, august

尊重	sonchō	value, respect, pay high regard to	227
自尊(心)	jison(shin)	self-respect, pride	62, 97
尊大	sondai	haughtiness, arrogance	26
本尊	honzon	Buddha; idol; he himself, she herself	25

705

夂 艹 口
4i 3k 3d

KEI, uyama(u) – respect, revere

尊敬	sonkei	respect, deference	704
敬意	keii	respect, homage	132
敬老	keirō	respect for the aged	543
敬遠	keien	keep at a respectful distance	446
敬語	keigo	an honorific, term of respect	67

706

言 夂 艹
7a 4i 3k

KEI – admonish, warn

警察	keisatsu	police	619
警官	keikan	policeman	326
警視	keishi	police superintendent	606
警告	keikoku	warning, admonition	690
警報	keihō	warning (signal), alarm	685

707	吐 一
	2e 3b 1a2

oro(su) – sell wholesale; **oroshi** – wholesaling

卸商	oroshishō	wholesaler	412
卸値	oroshine	wholesale price	425
卸し売り物価	oroshiuri bukka	wholesale prices	239, 79, 421

卸

708	彳 土 阝
	3i 3b 2e

GYO, GO, on- – (honorific prefix)

制御	seigyo	control, governing, suppression	427
御飯	gohan	boiled rice; meal	325
御用の方	goyō no kata	customer, inquirer	107, 70
御所	gosho	imperial palace	153
御中	onchū	Dear sirs:, Gentlemen:, Messrs.	28

御

709	力 口
	2g 3d

KA, kuwa(eru) – add, append; **kuwa(waru)** – join, take part (in)

加入	kanyū	joining	52
加工	kakō	processing	139
加法	kahō	addition (in mathematics)	123
倍加	baika	doubling	87
付加価値税	fukakachizei	value-added tax	192, 421, 425, 399

加

710	彡 亻 一
	3j 2a 1a

SAN – three (in documents); go, come, visit; **mai(ru)** – go, come, visit, visit a temple/shrine

参加	sanka	participation	709
参列	sanretsu	attendance, presence	611
参議院	Sangiin	(Japanese) House of Councilors	292, 614
参考書	sankōsho	reference book/work	541, 131

参

711	一 艹 ノ (1a) 3k 1c	**BEN** – speech, dialect; discrimination; petal; valve

弁当	*bentō*	box/sack lunch	77
駅弁	*ekiben*	box lunch sold at a train station	284
答弁	*tōben*	reply, answer	160
弁解一	*benkai*	explanation, justification, excuse	474
関西弁	*Kansai-ben*	Kansai dialect/accent	398, 72

712	土 田 日 3b 5f 4c	**ZŌ, ma(su), fu(eru)** – increase, rise; **fu(yasu)** – increase, raise

増加	*zōka*	increase, rise, growth	709
増産	*zōsan*	increase in production	278
増税	*zōzei*	tax increase	399
増進	*zōshin*	increase, furtherance, improvement	437

713	宀 田 口 3m 5f 3d	**FU, [FŪ], tomi** – wealth; **to(mu)** – be/become rich

国富	*kokufu*	national wealth	40
富強	*fukyō*	wealth and power	217
富力	*furyoku*	wealth, resources	100
富者	*fusha, fūsha*	rich person, the wealthy	164
富士山	*Fuji-san*	Mount Fuji	572, 34

714	刂 田 口 2f 5f 3d	**FUKU** – assistant, accompany, supplement

副社長	*fukushachō*	company vice-president	308, 95
副業	*fukugyō*	side business, sideline	279
副産物	*fukusanbutsu*	by-product	278, 79
副作用	*fukusayō*	side effects	360, 107
副題	*fukudai*	subtitle, subheading	354

715

氵 戈 口
3a 4n 3d

減

GEN, he(ru) – decrease, diminish; **he(rasu)** – decrease, shorten

増減	*zōgen*	increase and/or decrease	712
加減	*kagen*	addition and subtraction; state of health	709
減少	*genshō*	decrease, reduction	144
半減	*hangen*	reduction by half	88
減法	*genpō*	subtraction (in mathematics)	123

716

丷 皿 一
2o2 5h 1a

益

EKI, [YAKU] – profit, use, advantage

利益	*rieki*	profit, advantage	329
公益	*kōeki*	the public good	126
有益	*yūeki*	useful, beneficial, profitable	265
無益	*mueki*	useless, in vain	93
益鳥	*ekichō*	beneficial bird	285

717

皿 日 月
5h 4c 4b

盟

MEI – oath; alliance

連盟	*renmei*	league, federation	440
同盟	*dōmei*	alliance, confederation	198
加盟	*kamei*	joining affiliation	709
盟主	*meishu*	the leader, leading power	155
盟約	*meiyaku*	pledge, pact; alliance	211

718

言 戈 一
7a 4n 1a

誠

SEI, makoto – truth, reality; sincerity, fidelity

誠実	*seijitsu*	sincere, faithful, truthful	203
誠意	*seii*	sincerity, good faith	132
誠心誠意	*seishin-seii*	sincerely, wholeheartedly	97, 132
誠に	*makoto ni*	truly, indeed; sincerely; very	

719	皿 戈 一 5h 4n 1a	**SEI, [JŌ], saka(n)** – prosperous, energetic; **saka(ru)** – flourish, prosper; **mo(ru)** – serve (food); heap up

盛大	seidai	thriving, grand, magnificent	26
全盛	zensei	height of prosperity, zenith, heyday	89
最盛期	saiseiki	golden age, zenith	263, 449
花盛り	hanazakari	in full bloom, at its best	255

盛　盛　盛

盛　盛　盛

720	土 戈 一 3b 4n 1a	**JŌ, shiro** – castle

城下町	jōkamachi	castle town	31, 182
城主	jōshu	feudal lord of a castle	155
開城	kaijō	surrender of a fortress, capitulation	396
城門	jōmon	castle gate	161
古城	kojō	old castle	172

城　城　城

城　城　城

721	宀 口 ノ 3m 3d2 1c	**KYŪ, GŪ, [KU], miya** – shrine, palace, prince

宮城	kyūjō	imperial palace	720
神宮	jingū	Shinto shrine	310
宮参り	miyamairi	visit to a shrine	710
宮城県	Miyagi-ken	Miyagi Prefecture	720, 194
子宮	shikyū	uterus, womb	103

宮　宮　宮

宮　宮　宮

722	丷 口 冖 3n 3d2 2i	**EI, itona(mu)** – perform (a ceremony); conduct (business)

経営	keiei	management, administration	548
運営	un'ei	operation, management, running	439
公営	kōei	public management, municipally run	126
営業	eigyō	(running a) business	279
営利	eiri	profit, profit-making	329

営　営　営

営　営　営

723	⼱ 木 一 3n 4a 2i	**EI, ha(e)** – glory, honor, splendor; **ha(eru)** – shine, be brilliant; **saka(eru)** – thrive, prosper			
		栄養	eiyō	nutrition	402
		光栄	kōei	honor, glory	138
		栄光	eikō	glory	138
		見栄え	mibae	outward appearance	63

724	⼱ ⼱ 一 (2b) 3a 1a	**KYŪ, moto(meru)** – want; request, demand, seek			
		請求	seikyū	a claim, demand	661
		要求	yōkyū	demand	419
		求職	kyūshoku	seeking employment, job hunting	385
		求人	kyūjin	job offer, Help Wanted	1
		探求	tankyū	research, investigation	535

725	攵 ⼱ 一 4i 3a 1a	**KYŪ, suku(u)** – rescue, aid			
		救急	kyūkyū	first aid	303
		救助	kyūjo	rescue, relief	623
		救済	kyūsai	relief, aid, redemption, salvation	549
		救命ボート	kyūmei bōto	lifeboat	578
		救世軍	Kyūseigun	Salvation Army	252, 438

726	王 ⼱ 一 4f 3a 1a	**KYŪ, tama** – ball, sphere			
		野球	yakyū	baseball	236
		球場	kyūjō	baseball stadium, ball park	154
		電球	denkyū	light bulb	108
		(軽)気球	(kei)kikyū	(hot-air/helium) balloon	547, 134
		地球	chikyū	the earth, globe	118

727

	亻 王 戈
	2a 4f 4n

GI – rule; ceremony; affair, matter

礼儀	*reigi*	politeness, courtesy, propriety	620
礼儀正しい	*reigi tadashii*	courteous, decorous	620, 275
儀式	*gishiki*	ceremony, formality, ritual	525
儀典長	*gitenchō*	chief of protocol	367, 95
地球儀	*chikyūgi*	a globe	118, 726

儀　儀　儀

728

	牛 王 戈
	4g 4f 4n

GI – sacrifice

犠　犠　犠

729

	牛 土 一
	4g 3b 1a

SEI – sacrifice

| 犠牲 | *gisei* | sacrifice | 728 |
| 犠牲者 | *giseisha* | victim | 728, 164 |

牲　牲　牲

730

	日 土 一
	4c 3b 1a

SEI, [SHŌ], hoshi – star

火星	*kasei*	Mars	20
明星	*myōjō*	morning star, Venus	18
すい星	*suisei*	comet	
流れ星	*nagareboshi*	shooting star, meteor	247
星空	*hoshizora*	starry sky	140

星　星　星

731 牛 攵 (4g 4i)

BOKU, maki – pasture

牧場	bokujō, makiba	pasture, meadow	154
牧草地	bokusōchi	pasture, grassland, meadowland	249, 118
放牧	hōboku	pasturage, grazing	512
牧羊者	bokuyōsha	sheep raiser, shepherd	288, 164
牧師	bokushi	pastor, minister	409

732 亻 牛 (2a 4g)

KEN – matter, affair, case

事件	jiken	incident, affair, case	80
条件	jōken	condition, terms, stipulation	564
要件	yōken	important matter; condition, requisite	419
用件	yōken	(item of) business	107
案件	anken	matter, case, item	106

733 ⺈ 囗 丶 (2n 3s 2o)

MEN, manuka(reru) – escape, avoid, be exempt from

御免	gomen	pardon; declining, refusal	708
免責	menseki	exemption from responsibility	655
免税	menzei	tax exemption	399
免状	menjō	diploma; license	626
免職	menshoku	dismissal from one's job/office	385

734 辶 囗 ⺈ (2q 3s 2n)

ITSU – idleness; diverge, deviate from

逸話	itsuwa	anecdote	238
逸品	ippin	superb article, masterpiece	230
放逸	hōitsu	self-indulgence, licentiousness	512

735	⺈ 口 力
	2n 3s 2g

BEN – effort, hard work

勤 勉	*kinben*	industriousness, diligence, hard work	559
勉 強	*benkyō*	studying; diligence; sell cheap	217
勉 強 家	*benkyōka*	diligent student; hard worker	217, 165
勉 学	*bengaku*	study, pursuit of one's studies	109

勉　勉　勉

勉　勉　勉

736	日 口 ⺈
	4c 3s 2n

BAN – evening, night

今 晩	*konban*	this evening, tonight	51
毎 晩	*maiban*	every evening	116
一 晩	*hitoban*	a night, all night	2
朝 晩	*asaban*	mornings and evenings, day and night	469
晩 年	*bannen*	latter part of one's life	45

晩　晩　晩

晩　晩　晩

737	言 十 一
	7a 2k 1a

KYO, yuru(su) – permit, allow

免 許	*menkyo*	permission, license	733
許 可	*kyoka*	permission, approval, authorization	388
許 容	*kyoyō*	permission, tolerance	654
特 許	*tokkyo*	special permission; patent	282
特 許 法	*tokkyohō*	patent law	282, 123

許　許　許

許　許　許

738	言 心 刂
	7a 4k 2f

NIN, mito(meru) – perceive; recognize; approve of

認 可	*ninka*	approval	388
認 定	*nintei*	approval, acknowledgment	355
確 認	*kakunin*	confirmation, certification	603
公 認	*kōnin*	official recognition/sanction	126
認 識	*ninshiki*	cognition, recognition, perception	681

認　認　認

認　認　認

739 象 ⺈ 口 丨
2n 3s 1b

SHŌ – image, shape; **ZŌ** – elephant

具象的	*gushōteki*	concrete, embodied	420, 210
現象	*genshō*	phenomenon	298
対象	*taishō*	object, subject, target	365
気象学	*kishōgaku*	meteorology	134, 109
象げ	*zōge*	ivory	

740 像 亻 口 ⺈
2a 3s 2n

ZŌ – statue, image

仏像	*butsuzō*	statue/image of Buddha	583
自画像	*jigazō*	self-portrait	62, 343
受像機	*juzōki*	television set	260, 528
現像	*genzō*	(photographic) development	298
想像	*sōzō*	imagination	147

741 株 木 一 ノ
4a2 1a 1c

kabu – share, stock; stump

株式会社	*kabushiki-gaisha/kaisha*	Co., Ltd.	525, 158, 308
株券	*kabuken*	share, stock certificate	506
株主	*kabunushi*	stockholder	155
株主総会	*kabunushi sōkai*	general meeting of shareholders	155, 697, 158
切り株	*kirikabu*	(tree) stump, (grain) stubble	39

742 絶 糸 ⺈ 一
6a 2n 1a2

ZETSU, *ta(eru)* – die out, end; *ta(tsu)* – cut off, interrupt, eradicate; *ta(yasu)* – kill off, let die out

絶対	*zettai*	absolute	365
絶大	*zetsudai*	greatest, immense	26
絶望	*zetsubō*	despair	673
根絶	*konzetsu*	root out, eradicate, stamp out	314

743	糸 木 日 6a 4a 4c	**REN, *ne(ru)*** – knead; train; polish up		
		練習	renshū	practice, exercise	591
		教練	kyōren	(military) drill	245
		試練	shiren	trial, test, ordeal	526
		熟練	jukuren	practiced skill, expertness, mastery	687
		洗練	senren	polish, refine	692

練　練　練

練　練　練

744	日 亻 一 4c 2a2 1a4	**TAI, *ka(eru)*** – replace; ***ka(waru)*** – be replaced		
		代替	daitai	substitution	256
		両替	ryōgae	exchanging/changing money	200
		取り替え	torikae	exchange, swap, replacement	65
		切り替え	kirikae	renewal, changeover	39
		着替える	kigaeru, kikaeru	change clothes	657

替　替　替

替　替　替

745	貝 亻 一 7b 2a2 1a4	**SAN** – praise; agreement		
		賛成	sansei	agreement, approbation	261
		賛助	sanjo	support, backing	623
		協賛	kyōsan	approval, consent, support	234
		賞賛	shōsan	praise, admiration	500
		賛美	sanbi	praise, glorification	401

賛　賛　賛

賛　賛　賛

746	声 厂 一 3p 2p 1a	**SEI, [SHŌ], koe, [kowa-]** – voice		
		声明	seimei	declaration, statement, proclamation	18
		名声	meisei	fame, renown, reputation	82
		音声学	onseigaku	phonetics	347, 109
		声変わり	koegawari	change/cracking of voice	257
		声色	kowairo	imitated/assumed voice	204

声　声　声

声　声　声

747	⺮ 目 艹
	6f 5c 3k

SAN – calculate

計算	keisan	calculation, computation	340
公算	kōsan	probability, likelihood	126
予算	yosan	an estimate; budget	393
精算	seisan	exact calculation, (fare) adjustment	659
暗算	anzan	mental arithmetic/calculation	348

算　算　算　算

748	貝 戈 亻
	7b 4n 2a

TAI, ka(su) – rent out

貸与	taiyo	lend, loan	539
貸し家	kashiya	house for rent, rented house	165
貸しボート	kashibōto	boat for rent, rented boat	
貸し出す	kashidasu	lend/hire out	53
貸し切り	kashikiri	reservations, booking	39

貸　貸　貸　貸

749	貝 弓 丨
	7b 3h 1b2

HI, tsui(yasu) – spend; **tsui(eru)** – be wasted

経費	keihi	expenses, cost	548
費用	hiyō	expense, cost	107
生活費	seikatsuhi	living expenses, cost of living	44, 237
光熱費	kōnetsuhi	heating and lighting expenses	138, 645
旅費	ryohi	traveling expenses	222

費　費　費　費

750	貝 欠 冫
	7b 4j 2b

SHI – resources, capital, funds

資源	shigen	resources	580
資本	shihon	capital	25
資金	shikin	funds	23
物資	busshi	goods, (raw) materials	79
資格	shikaku	qualification, competence	643

資　資　資　資

751	貝 土 亻
	7b 3p 2a

CHIN – rent, wages, fare, fee

賃金	chingin	wages, pay	23
賃上げ	chin'age	raise in wages	32
運賃	unchin	passenger fare; shipping charges	439
電車賃	denshachin	train fare	108, 133
家賃	yachin	rent	165

752	貝 亻 卜
	7b 2a 2m

KA – freight; goods, property

貨物	kamotsu	freight	79
百貨店	hyakkaten	department store	14, 168
通貨	tsūka	currency	150
外貨	gaika	foreign goods/currency	83
銀貨	ginka	silver coin	313

753	貝 丶 刂
	7b 2o 2f

HIN, BIN, mazu(shii) – poor

貧富	hinpu	poverty and wealth, the rich and poor	713
貧困	hinkon	poverty, need	558
貧弱	hinjaku	poor, meager, scanty	218
貧相	hinsō	poor-looking, seedy	146
清貧	seihin	honest poverty	660

754	一 丨 ノ
	1a 1b 1c

BŌ, tobo(shii) – scanty, meager, scarce

| 貧乏 | binbō | poor | 753 |
| 欠乏 | ketsubō | shortage, deficiency | 383 |

755	木 口 力 4a 3d 2g	**KA, ka(keru)** – hang, build (bridge); **ka(karu)** – hang, be built		
		架設	*kasetsu*	construction, laying	577
		架橋	*kakyō*	bridge building	597
		書架	*shoka*	bookshelf	131
		十字架像	*jūjikazō*	crucifix	12, 110, 740
		架空	*kakū*	overhead, aerial; fanciful	140

架

架 架 架

架 架 架

756	貝 口 力 7b 3d 2g	**GA** – congratulations, felicitations		
		賀状	*gajō*	greeting card	626
		年賀	*nenga*	New Year's greetings	45
		年賀状	*nengajō*	New Year's card	45, 626
		賀正	*gashō*	New Year's greetings	275
		志賀高原	*Shiga Kōgen*	Shiga Highlands	573, 190, 136

賀

賀 賀 賀

賀 賀 賀

757	又 丨 2h 1b2	**SHŪ, osa(meru)** – obtain, collect; **osa(maru)** – be obtained, end		
		収支	*shūshi*	income and expenditures	318
		収入	*shūnyū*	income, earnings, receipts	52
		買収	*baishū*	purchase; buying off, bribery	241
		収益	*shūeki*	earnings, proceeds, profit	716
		収容	*shūyō*	admission, accommodation	654

収

収 収 収

収 収 収

758	糸 冂 イ 6a 2r 2a	**NŌ, [TŌ], [NA], [NA'], [NAN], osa(meru)** – pay; supply; accept, store; **osa(maru)** – be paid (in), supplied		
		納税	*nōzei*	payment of taxes	399
		出納	*suitō*	receipts and disbursements	53
		納得	*nattoku*	consent, understanding	374
		納屋	*naya*	(storage) shed	167

納

納 納 納

納 納 納

759	日 一 ノ 4c 1a 1c3	**EKI** – divination; **I, yasa(shii)** – easy		
		易者　　　　*ekisha*　　　fortune-teller　　　　　　　　　164		
		不易　　　　*fueki*　　　　immutability, unchangeableness　94		
		交易　　　　*kōeki*　　　　trade, commerce, barter　　　114		
		容易　　　　*yōi*　　　　　easy, simple　　　　　　　　654		
		難易 (度)　*nan'i(do)*　(degree of) difficulty　557, 377		

760	貝 刂 厂 7b 2f 2p	**BŌ** – exchange, trade		
		貿易　　　　　*bōeki*　　　　trade　　　　　　　　　　　759		
		自由貿易　　*jiyū bōeki*　　free trade　　　　　62, 363, 759		
		貿易会社　　*bōeki-gaisha*　trading firm/company　759, 158, 308		
		貿易収支　　*bōeki shūshi*　balance of trade　759, 757, 318		
		日米貿易　*Nichi-Bei bōeki*　Japan-U.S. trade　5, 224, 759		

761	田 刂 厂 5f 2f 2p	**RYŪ, [RU], to(meru)** – fasten down; hold, keep (in); **to(maru)** – stay, settle		
		留学　　　　*ryūgaku*　　　study abroad　　　　　　　109		
		留守　　　　*rusu*　　　　　absence from home　　　　490		
		書留　　　　*kakitome*　　　registered mail　　　　　131		
		局留 (め)　*kyokudome*　　general delivery　　　　　170		

762	貝 宀 一 7b 3m 1a	**CHO** – storage		
		貯金　　　　*chokin*　　　　savings, deposit　　　　　23		
		貯水池　　　*chosuichi*　　reservoir　　　　　　　21, 119		

763	广 一 丨 3q 1a 1b	**CHŌ** – government office, agency	
		官庁 kanchō government office, agency	326
		警視庁 Keishichō Metropolitan Police Department	706, 606
		気象庁 Kishōchō Meteorological Agency	134, 739
		県庁 kenchō prefectural office	194

庁

764	艹 日 一 3k 4c 1a	**SEKI, [SHAKU], mukashi** – antiquity, long ago	
		今昔 konjaku past and present	51
		大昔 ōmukashi remote antiquity, time immemorial	26
		昔々 mukashimukashi Once upon a time ...	
		昔話 mukashibanashi old tale, legend	238
		昔の事 mukashi no koto thing of the past	80

昔

765	心 日 艹 4k 4c 3k	**SEKI, o(shii)** – regrettable; precious; wasteful; **o(shimu)** – regret; value; begrudge, be sparing of	
		惜敗 sekihai narrow defeat (after a hard-fought contest)	511
		愛惜 aiseki be loath to part	259
		口惜しい kuchioshii regrettable, vexing	54
		負け惜しみ makeoshimi unwillingness to admit defeat	510

惜

766	亻 日 艹 2a 4c 3k	**SHAKU, ka(riru)** – borrow, rent	
		借金 shakkin debt	23
		借財 shakuzai debt	553
		貸借 taishaku debits and credits	748
		転借 tenshaku subleasing	433
		賃借/借り chin-shaku/gari lease	751

借

| 767 | 夂月 艹
4i 4b 3k | **SAN**, *chi(rakasu)* – scatter, disarrange; *chi(rakaru)* – lie scattered, be in disorder; *chi(ru/rasu)* – (intr./tr.) scatter |

解 散	*kaisan*	breakup, dissolution, disbanding	474
散 会	*sankai*	adjournment	158
散 文	*sanbun*	prose	111
散 歩	*sanpo*	walk, stroll	431

| 768 | 亻 艹 冂
2a 3k 2r | **BI**, *sona(eru)* – furnish, provide (for); *sona(waru)* – possess |

設 備	*setsubi*	equipment, facilities	577
整 備	*seibi*	maintenance, servicing	503
軍 備	*gunbi*	military preparations, armaments	438
予 備 費	*yobihi*	reserves, reserve funds	393, 749
備 考	*bikō*	explanatory notes, remarks	541

| 769 | 頁 丨
9a 1b3 | **JUN** – order, sequence |

順 番	*junban*	order, one's turn	185
順 位	*jun'i*	ranking, standing	122
語 順	*gojun*	word order	67
五 十 音 順	*gojū-on jun*	in order of the kana syllabary	7, 12, 347
順 調	*junchō*	favorable, smooth, without a hitch	342

| 770 | 广 一 丨
3q 1a2 1b | **JO** – beginning; preface; order, precedence |

順 序	*junjo*	order, method, procedure	769
序 説	*josetsu*	introduction, preface	400
序 論	*joron*	introduction, preface	293
序 文	*jobun*	preface, foreword, introduction	111
序 曲	*jokyoku*	overture, prelude	366

771 訓 言丨 (7a 1b3)

KUN – Japanese reading of a kanji; teaching, precept

訓育	kun'iku	education, discipline	246
教訓	kyōkun	teaching, precept, moral	245
訓練	kunren	training	743
訓辞	kunji	an admonitory speech, instructions	688
音訓	on-kun	Chinese and Japanese readings	347

772 盾 目 厂 十 (5c 2p 2k)

JUN, tate – shield

後ろ盾	ushirodate	support, backing, supporter, backer	48

773 矛 一 丨 ノ (1a2 1b 1c)

MU, hoko – halberd

矛盾	mujun	contradiction	772
矛先	hokosaki	point of a spear; aim of an attack	50

774 柔 朩 一 丨 (4a 1a2 1b)

JŪ, NYŪ, yawa(rakai/raka) – soft

柔道	jūdō	judo	149
柔術	jūjutsu	jujitsu	187
柔弱	nyūjaku	weakness, enervation	218
柔和	nyūwa	gentle, mild(-mannered)	124
物柔らか	monoyawaraka	mild(-mannered), quiet, gentle	79

775	辶 刂 2q 2f	**HEN, ata(ri), -be** – vicinity			
		近辺	kinpen	neighborhood, vicinity	445
		周辺	shūhen	periphery, environs	91
		辺地	henchi	remote/out-of-the-way place	118
		多辺地	tahenchi	polygon	229, 395
		海辺	umibe	beach, seashore	117

辺 辺 辺

776	辶 ノ 丶 2q 1c 1d	**ko(mu)** – be crowded, congested; **ko(meru)** – include, count in; load (a gun); concentrate			
		巻き込む	makikomu	entangle, involve, implicate	507
		払い込む	haraikomu	pay in	582
		申し込み	mōshikomi	proposal, offer, application	309
		見込み	mikomi	prospects, outlook	63

込 込 込

777	辶 ノ 2q 1c3	**JUN, megu(ru)** – go around			
		巡回	junkai	tour, patrol, one's rounds	90
		巡視	junshi	tour of inspection, round of visits	606
		巡査	junsa	policeman, cop	624
		巡礼	junrei	pilgrimage, pilgrim	620
		巡業	jungyō	tour (of a troupe/team)	279

巡 巡 巡

778	十 隹 氵 2k 8c 3a	**JUN** – semi-, quasi-; level; correspond (to)			
		水準	suijun	water level; level, standard	21
		基準	kijun	standard, criterion	450
		規準	kijun	criterion, standard, norm	607
		準備	junbi	preparation	768
		準決勝	junkesshō	semifinal game/round	356, 509

準 準 準

INDEX by Readings
(Kanji 1 – 778)

– D –

Reading	Kanji	No.
DAI	内	84
	代	256
	弟	405
	台	492
	大	26
	題	354
	第	404
DAN	団	491
	暖	635
	段	362
	男	101
	談	593
da(su)	出	53
DE	弟	405
DEN	伝	434
	田	35
	電	108
de(ru)	出	53
DO	土	24
	度	377
DŌ	働	232
	同	198
	動	231
	導	703
	堂	496
	童	410
	道	149
DOKU	毒	522
	独	219
	読	244
DON	畳	637

– E –

Reading	Kanji	No.
E	会	158
	依	678
	回	90
	絵	345
-e	重	227
EI	営	722
	映	352
	栄	723
	英	353
EKI	益	716
	役	375
	易	759
	液	472
	駅	284
EN	円	13
	園	447
	宴	640
	演	344
	遠	446
e(ru)	得	374

– F –

Reading	Kanji	No.
FU	不	94
	夫	315
	付	192
	婦	316
	富	713
	布	675
	府	504
	父	113
	符	505
	負	510
	風	29
	歩	431
	夫	315
FŪ	富	713
	風	29
fude	筆	130
fu(eru)	増	712
fuka(i)	深	536
fuka(maru)	深	536
fuka(meru)	深	536
fu(keru)	老	543
FUKU	副	714
	服	683
fumi	文	111
FUN	分	38
funa	船	376
fune	船	376
furu(i)	古	172
furu(su)	古	172
fuse(gu)	防	513
fushi	節	464
futa	二	3
futa(tsu)	二	3
futo(i)	太	629
futo(ru)	太	629
FUTSU	払	582
fu(yasu)	増	712
fuyu	冬	459

– G –

Reading	Kanji	No.
GA	画	343
	賀	756
GA'	合	159
GAI	外	83
	害	518
	街	186
	学	109
GAKU	楽	358
GAN	丸	644
	願	581
	元	137
	岸	586
	顔	277
GATSU	月	17
GE	下	31
	夏	461
	外	83
	解	474
GEI	芸	435
	鯨	700
GEN	元	137
	原	136
	減	715
	源	580
	現	298
	言	66
	験	532

Reading	Kanji	No.
GETSU	月	17
GI	儀	727
	犠	728
	義	291
	議	292
GIN	銀	313
GO	五	7
	午	49
	後	48
	御	708
	期	449
	語	67
GŌ	業	279
	合	159
	号	266
	強	217
GOKU	極	336
GON	勤	559
	権	335
	言	66
GU	具	420
GŪ	宮	721
GUN	軍	438
	郡	193
GYAKU	逆	444
GYO	御	708
	漁	699
	魚	290
	業	279
GYŌ	形	395
	行	68
GYOKU	玉	295
GYŪ	牛	281

– H –

Reading	Kanji	No.
HA	波	666
	破	665
HA'	法	123
ha	羽	590
	葉	253
	歯	478
	省	145
HACHI	八	10
ha(e)	栄	723
ha(eru)	映	352
	栄	723
	生	44
haha	母	112
HAI	敗	511
	配	515
hai(ru)	入	52
haji(maru)	始	494
haji(me)	初	679
haji(meru)	始	494
haji(mete)	初	679
haka(rau)	計	340
haka(ru)	図	339
	量	411
	測	610
	計	340
hako(bu)	運	439
HAKU	博	601
	白	205

Reading	Kanji	No.
HAN	半	88
	反	324
	坂	443
	飯	325
hana	花	255
hana(reru)	放	512
hanashi	話	238
hana(su)	放	512
	話	238
hana(tsu)	放	512
hane	羽	590
hara	原	136
ha(rasu)	晴	662
hara(u)	払	582
ha(reru)	晴	662
hari	針	341
haru	春	460
hashi	橋	597
hashira	柱	598
hashi(ru)	走	429
hata	機	528
	畑	36
hatake	畑	36
hatara(ku)	働	232
ha(tasu)	果	487
ha(te)	果	487
ha(teru)	果	487
HATSU	発	96
hatsu-	初	679
haya(i)	早	248
	速	502
haya(maru)	早	248
haya(meru)	早	248
	速	502
hayashi	林	127
ha(yasu)	生	44
hazu(reru)	外	83
hazu(su)	外	83
HEI	平	202
	病	380
	閉	397
	陛	589
HEN	変	257
	編	682
	辺	775
	返	442
he(rasu)	減	715
he(ru)	減	715
	経	548
HI	費	749
	非	498
	飛	530
hi	日	5
	火	20
hidari	左	75
higashi	東	71
hikari	光	138
hika(ru)	光	138
hi(keru)	引	216
hi(ku)	引	216
hiku(i)	低	561
hiku(maru)	低	561
hiku(meru)	低	561
HIN	貧	753

Reading	Kanji	Page
kawa	買	241
	側	609
	川	33
	河	389
ka(waru)	変	257
	代	256
	替	744
ka(wasu)	交	114
kayo(u)	通	150
kaza-	風	29
kaze	風	29
kazo(eru)	数	225
kazu	数	225
KE	化	254
	家	165
	気	134
ke	毛	287
kega-(rawashii)	汚	693
kega(reru)	汚	693
kega(su)	汚	693
KEI	京	189
	兄	406
	契	565
	形	395
	敬	705
	経	548
	計	340
	警	706
	軽	547
KEN	件	732
	券	506
	圏	508
	憲	521
	県	194
	検	531
	権	335
	犬	280
	見	63
	険	533
	験	532
	間	43
KETSU	欠	383
	決	356
	結	485
kewa(shii)	険	533
KI	危	534
	企	481
	器	527
	基	450
	己	370
	希	676
	帰	317
	機	528
	気	134
	汽	135
	祈	621
	季	465
	紀	372
	期	449
	規	607
	記	371
	起	373
ki	木	22
ki-	生	44
ki(koeru)	聞	64
KIKU	菊	475
ki(ku)	利	329
	聞	64
	決	356
ki(meru)	決	356
KIN	今	51
	勤	559
	禁	482
	近	445
	金	23
ki(reru)	切	39
ki(ru)	切	39
	着	657
ki(seru)	着	657
kishi	岸	586
kita	北	73
kitana(i)	汚	693
kita(ru)	来	69
kita(su)	来	69
KIWA	際	618
kiwa(maru)	極	336
kiwa(meru)	極	336
kiwa(mi)	極	336
kiyo(i)	清	660
kiyo(maru)	清	660
kiyo(meru)	清	660
kizu	傷	633
KO	古	172
	去	414
	己	370
	戸	152
	故	173
	湖	467
	子	103
	木	22
	小	27
ko-	向	199
KŌ	交	114
	公	126
	興	368
	孝	542
	厚	639
	口	54
	幸	684
	好	104
	光	138
	工	139
	広	694
	後	48
	格	643
	校	115
	港	669
	皇	297
	考	541
	行	68
	高	190
kō	神	310
koe	声	746
koi	恋	258
koi(shii)	恋	258
kokono	九	11
kokono(tsu)	九	11
kokoro	心	97
kokoro(miru)	試	526
kokorozashi	志	573
kokoroza(su)	志	573
KOKU	告	690
	国	40
	谷	653
	黒	206
	石	78
koma(ka)	細	695
koma(kai)	細	695
koma(ru)	困	558
kome	米	224
ko(meru)	込	776
ko(mu)	込	776
KON	今	51
	困	558
	婚	567
	根	314
	金	23
kono(mu)	好	104
koro(bu)	転	433
koro(garu)	転	433
koro(gasu)	転	433
koro(geru)	転	433
koromo	衣	677
koro(su)	殺	576
kota(e)	答	160
kota(eru)	答	160
koto	事	80
-koto	言	66
ko(u)	恋	258
	請	661
kowa-	声	746
KU	九	11
	供	197
	句	337
	区	183
	口	54
	宮	721
	工	139
	苦	545
KŪ	空	140
	配	515
kuba(ru)	配	515
kubi	首	148
kuchi	口	54
kuda	管	328
kuda(ru)	下	31
kuda(saru)	下	31
kuda(su)	下	31
kujira	鯨	700
kumi	組	418
kumo	雲	636
kumo(ru)	曇	637
ku(mu)	組	418
KUN	訓	771
kuni	国	40
kurai	位	122
kura(i)	暗	348
ku(rau)	食	322
kuro	黒	206
kuro(i)	黒	206
ku(ru)	来	69
kuruma	車	133
kuru(shii)	苦	545
kuru(shimeru)	苦	545
kuru(shimu)	苦	545
kusa	草	249
kusuri	薬	359
ku(u)	食	322
kuwada(teru)	企	481
kuwa(eru)	加	709
kuwa(waru)	加	709
KYAKU	客	641
KYO	去	414
	居	171
	許	737
KYŌ	京	189
	供	197
	共	196
	興	368
	協	234
	兄	406
	強	217
	教	245
	橋	597
	経	548
KYOKU	曲	366
	局	170
	極	336
KYŪ	求	724
	九	11
	休	60
	宮	721
	弓	212
	急	303
	救	725
	球	726
	級	568
	給	346

– M –

Reading	Kanji	Page
ma	目	55
	間	43
	真	422
	馬	283
machi	街	186
	町	182
mado	窓	698
mae	前	47
ma(garu)	曲	366
ma(geru)	曲	366
MAI	妹	408
	毎	116
	米	224
mai(ru)	参	710
maji(eru)	交	114
ma(jiru)	交	114
maji(waru)	交	114
maka(seru)	任	334
maka(su)	任	334
ma(kasu)	負	510
ma(keru)	負	510
maki	巻	507
	牧	731
makoto	誠	718
ma(ku)	巻	507

Reading	漢字	No.
mamo(ru)	守	490
MAN	万	16
	満	201
mana(bu)	学	109
mane(ku)	招	455
manuka(reru)	免	733
maru	丸	644
maru(i)	丸	644
	円	13
maru(meru)	丸	644
masa(ni)	正	275
masa(ru)	勝	509
ma(su)	増	712
mato	的	210
MATSU	末	305
matsu	松	696
ma(tsu)	待	452
matsu(ri)	祭	617
matsurigoto	政	483
matsu(ru)	祭	617
matta(ku)	全	89
mawa(ri)	周	91
mawa(ru)	回	90
mawa(su)	回	90
ma(zaru)	交	114
ma(zeru)	交	114
mazu(shii)	貧	753
me	目	55
	女	102
megu(ru)	巡	777
MEI	命	578
	名	82
	明	18
	盟	717
MEN	免	733
	面	274
meshi	飯	325
MI	未	306
	味	307
mi	三	4
	実	203
	身	59
michi	道	149
michibi(ku)	導	703
mi(chiru)	満	201
mida(reru)	乱	689
mida(su)	乱	689
midori	緑	537
mi(eru)	見	63
migi	右	76
mijika(i)	短	215
mimi	耳	56
MIN	民	177
mina	皆	587
minami	南	74
minamoto	源	580
minato	港	669
mino(ru)	実	203
mi(ru)	見	63
mise	店	168
mi(seru)	見	63
mi(tasu)	満	201
mito(meru)	認	738
mi(tsu)	三	4
mit(tsu)	三	4
miya	宮	721
miyako	都	188
mizu	水	21
mizuka(ra)	自	62
mizuumi	湖	467
MŌ	亡	672
	毛	287
	望	673
mochi(iru)	用	107
mo(eru)	燃	652
mō(keru)	設	577
MOKU	木	22
	目	55
MON	文	111
	門	161
	問	162
	聞	64
mono	物	79
	者	164
moppa(ra)	専	600
mori	守	490
	森	128
	盛	719
mo(ru)	盛	719
mo(shikuwa)	若	544
mo(su)	燃	652
mō(su)	申	309
moto	下	31
	本	25
	元	137
	基	450
motoi	基	450
moto(meru)	求	724
MOTSU	物	79
mo(tsu)	持	451
motto(mo)	最	263
mo(yasu)	燃	652
MU	無	93
	矛	773
	務	235
mu	六	8
mugi	麦	270
mui	六	8
mukashi	昔	764
mu(kau)	向	199
mu(keru)	向	199
mu(kō)	向	199
mu(ku)	向	199
muku(iru)	報	685
mura	村	191
muro	室	166
musu(bu)	結	485
mu(tsu)	六	8
mut(tsu)	六	8
muzuka(shii)	難	557
MYŌ	命	578
	名	82
	明	18

– N –

Reading	漢字	No.
NA	南	74
	納	758
NA'	納	758
na	名	82
naga(i)	長	95
naga(reru)	流	247
naga(su)	流	247
nago(mu)	和	124
nago(yaka)	和	124
NAI	内	84
na(i)	亡	672
	無	93
naka	中	28
naka(ba)	半	88
nama	生	44
nami	波	666
NAN	南	74
	男	101
	納	758
	難	557
nan	何	390
nana	七	9
nana(tsu)	七	9
nani	何	390
nano	七	9
nao(ru)	直	423
	治	493
nao(su)	直	423
	治	493
nara(u)	習	591
na(ru)	成	261
nasa(ke)	情	209
na(su)	成	261
natsu	夏	461
ne	値	425
	根	314
	音	347
nega(u)	願	581
NEN	年	45
	念	579
	然	651
	燃	652
	練	743
ne(ru)	練	743
NETSU	熱	645
NI	二	3
ni	荷	391
NICHI	日	5
niga(i)	苦	545
niga(ru)	苦	545
nii-	新	174
NIKU	肉	223
NIN	人	1
	任	334
	認	738
nishi	西	72
no	野	236
NŌ	能	386
	納	758
	農	369
nobo(ru)	上	32
nobo(seru)	上	32
nobo(su)	上	32
nochi	後	48
noko(ru)	残	650
noko(su)	残	650
no(mu)	飲	323
no(ru)	乗	523
no(seru)	乗	523
nozo(mu)	望	673
nuno	布	675
nushi	主	155
NYAKU	若	544
NYO	女	102
NYŌ	女	102
NYŪ	入	52
	柔	774

– O –

Reading	漢字	No.
O	悪	304
	汚	693
	和	124
o-	小	27
Ō	央	351
	奥	476
	王	294
	皇	297
ō-	大	26
obo(eru)	覚	605
o(eru)	終	458
ō(i)	多	229
ō(ini)	大	26
o(iru)	老	543
ō(kii)	大	26
o(kiru)	起	373
okona(u)	行	68
oko(ru)	興	368
o(koru)	起	373
oko(su)	興	368
o(kosu)	起	373
OKU	億	382
	屋	167
	憶	381
oku	奥	476
o(ku)	置	426
oku(rasu)	遅	702
oku(reru)	後	48
	遅	702
oku(ru)	送	441
omo	主	155
	面	274
	重	227
omo(i)	重	227
omote	表	272
	面	274
omo(u)	思	99
ON	恩	555
	温	634
	遠	446
	音	347
on-	御	708
ona(ji)	同	198
onna	女	102
onoono	各	642
onore	己	370
o(riru)	下	31
oroshi	卸	707
oro(su)	卸	707
	下	31
o(ru)	織	680
osa(maru)	収	757
	治	493

Reading	Kanji	No.
	城	720
shiro(i)	白	205
	白	205
shi(ru)	知	214
shiru(su)	記	371
shita	下	31
shita(shii)	親	175
shita(shimu)	親	175
SHITSU	失	311
	執	686
	室	166
	質	176
shizu	静	663
shizu(ka)	静	663
shizu(maru)	静	663
shizu(meru)	静	663
SHO	所	153
	暑	638
	書	131
	初	679
SHŌ	正	275
	少	144
	省	145
	商	412
	傷	633
	上	32
	声	746
	小	27
	掌	499
	賞	500
	性	98
	招	455
	政	483
	星	730
	松	696
	相	146
	渉	432
	清	660
	将	627
	生	44
	精	659
	紹	456
	勝	509
	証	484
	象	739
	青	208
	植	424
SHOKU	織	680
	職	385
	色	204
	食	322
SHU	主	155
	守	490
	手	57
	酒	517
	種	228
	取	65
	首	148
SHŪ	州	195
	周	91
	収	757
	執	686
	宗	616
	秋	462

Reading	Kanji	No.
	終	458
	習	591
	週	92
	集	436
SHUKU	宿	179
SHUN	春	460
SHUTSU	出	53
SO	想	147
	相	622
	素	271
	組	418
	争	302
SŌ	宗	616
	想	147
	早	248
	相	146
	窓	698
	総	697
	草	249
	走	429
	送	441
	育	246
soda(teru)	育	246
soda(tsu)	育	246
soko	底	562
soko(nau)	損	350
soko(neru)	損	350
SOKU	束	501
	側	609
	測	610
	即	463
	則	608
	足	58
	速	502
	初	679
-so(meru)	尊	704
SON	存	269
	損	350
	村	191
sona(eru)	供	197
	備	768
sona(waru)	備	768
sono	園	447
sora	空	140
	反	324
so(rasu)	反	324
so(ru)	注	357
soso(gu)	外	83
soto	主	155
SU	子	103
	守	490
	数	225
	素	271
	州	195
su	数	225
SŪ	末	305
sue	過	413
su(giru)	過	413
su(gosu)	出	53
SUI	水	21
su(i)	酸	516
suke	助	623
suko(shi)	少	144
su(ku)	好	104
suku(nai)	少	144

Reading	Kanji	No.
suku(u)	救	725
su(masu)	済	549
su(mau)	住	156
sumi(yaka)	速	502
su(mu)	住	156
su(mu)	済	549
susu(meru)	進	437
susu(mu)	進	437

– T –

Reading	Kanji	No.
TA	他	120
	多	229
	太	629
ta	手	57
	田	35
taba	束	501
ta(beru)	食	322
tabi	度	377
	旅	222
tada(chini)	直	423
tada(shii)	正	275
tada(su)	正	275
ta(eru)	絶	742
TAI	代	256
	体	61
	台	492
	大	26
	太	629
	待	452
	態	387
	対	365
	替	744
	貸	748
tai(ra)	平	202
taka	高	190
taka(i)	高	190
taka(maru)	高	190
taka(meru)	高	190
takara	宝	296
take	竹	129
TAKU	宅	178
	度	377
tama	玉	295
	球	726
tame(su)	試	526
tami	民	177
tamo(tsu)	保	489
TAN	単	300
	探	535
	短	215
	反	324
tane	種	228
tani	谷	653
tano(shii)	楽	358
tano(shimu)	楽	358
ta(riru)	足	58
ta(ru)	足	58
tashi(ka)	確	603
tashi(kameru)	確	603
ta(su)	足	58
tasu(karu)	助	623
tasu(keru)	助	623
tataka(u)	戦	301

Reading	Kanji	No.
tate	盾	772
	立	121
ta(teru)	例	612
TATSU	達	448
ta(tsu)	立	121
	絶	742
tatto(bu)	尊	704
tatto(i)	尊	704
ta(yasu)	絶	742
tayo(ri)	便	330
te	手	57
TEI	丁	184
	体	61
	低	561
	弟	405
	定	355
	底	562
	抵	560
	提	628
	程	417
	邸	563
TEKI	敵	416
	的	210
	適	415
TEN	天	141
	典	367
	点	169
	店	168
	転	433
tera	寺	41
TETSU	鉄	312
TO	図	339
	土	24
	度	377
	徒	430
	渡	378
	頭	276
	都	188
to	十	12
	戸	152
TŌ	東	71
	島	286
	刀	37
	冬	459
	当	77
	党	495
	湯	632
	答	160
	等	569
	納	758
	読	244
	頭	276
	道	149
to(basu)	飛	530
tobo(shii)	乏	754
to(bu)	飛	530
to(i)	問	162
tō(i)	遠	446
to(jiru)	閉	397
to(kasu)	解	474
to(keru)	解	474
toki	時	42
toko-	常	497

Reading	Kanji	Page
tokoro	所	153
TOKU	得	374
	特	282
	読	244
to(ku)	解	474
	説	400
to(maru)	止	477
	留	761
to(meru)	止	477
	留	761
tomi	富	713
tomo	供	197
	共	196
	友	264
to(mu)	富	713
TON	団	491
ton	問	162
tori	鳥	285
to(ru)	執	686
	取	65
tō(ru)	通	150
toshi	年	45
tō(su)	通	150
tōto(bu)	尊	704
tōto(i)	尊	704
totono(eru)	整	503
	調	342
totono(u)	整	503
	調	342
to(u)	問	162
to(zasu)	閉	397
TSU	通	150
	都	188
tsu	津	668
TSŪ	通	150
tsuchi	土	24
tsudo(u)	集	436
tsu(geru)	告	690
tsugi	次	384
tsu(gu)	次	384
	接	486
TSUI	対	365
tsui(eru)	費	749
tsui(yasu)	費	749
tsuka(eru)	仕	333
tsuka(u)	使	331
tsu(keru)	付	192
	着	657
tsuki	月	17
tsu(ku)	付	192
	着	657
tsuku(ru)	作	360
	造	691
tsuma	妻	671
tsu(moru)	積	656
tsu(mu)	積	656
tsune	常	497
tsuno	角	473
tsura	面	274
tsura(naru)	連	440
tsura(neru)	連	440
tsu(reru)	連	440
tsuta(eru)	伝	434
tsuta(u)	伝	434
tsuta(waru)	伝	434
tsuto(maru)	勤	559
tsuto(meru)	勤	559
	務	235
tsuyo(i)	強	217
tsuyo(maru)	強	217
tsuyo(meru)	強	217
tsuzu(keru)	続	243
tsuzu(ku)	続	243

– U –

Reading	Kanji	Page
U	右	76
	羽	590
	有	265
	雨	30
ubu	産	278
uchi	内	84
ue	上	32
u(eru)	植	424
ugo(kasu)	動	231
ugo(ku)	動	231
ui-	初	679
uji	氏	566
u(karu)	受	260
u(keru)	受	260
	請	661
uma	馬	283
	生	44
u(mareru)	産	278
umi	海	117
u(mu)	生	44
	産	278
UN	運	439
	雲	636
uo	魚	290
ura	裏	273
u(reru)	売	239
	熟	687
u(ru)	売	239
	得	374
ushi	牛	281
ushina(u)	失	311
ushi(ro)	後	48
uta	歌	392
uta(u)	歌	392
utsuku(shii)	美	401
utsu(ru)	写	540
	映	352
utsu(su)	写	540
	映	352
utsuwa	器	527
uwa-	上	32
u(waru)	植	424
uyama(u)	敬	705

– W –

Reading	Kanji	Page
WA	和	124
	話	238
waka(i)	若	544
waka(reru)	別	267
wa(kareru)	分	38
wa(karu)	分	38
wa(katsu)	分	38
wake	訳	594
wa(keru)	分	38
WAN	湾	670
warabe	童	410
wa(reru)	割	519
wari	割	519
wa(ru)	割	519
waru(i)	悪	304
watakushi	私	125
wata(ru)	渡	378
wata(su)	渡	378
waza	業	279

– Y –

Reading	Kanji	Page
YA	夜	471
	野	236
ya	八	10
	屋	167
	矢	213
	家	165
yabu(reru)	破	665
	敗	511
yabu(ru)	破	665
yado	宿	179
yado(ru)	宿	179
yado(su)	宿	179
YAKU	益	716
	役	375
	約	211
	薬	359
	訳	594
yama	山	34
yamai	病	380
ya(meru)	辞	688
ya(mu)	病	380
yasa(shii)	易	759
yashina(u)	養	402
yashiro	社	308
yasu(i)	安	105
yasu(maru)	休	60
yasu(meru)	休	60
yasu(mu)	休	60
ya(tsu)	八	10
yat(tsu)	八	10
yawa(rageru)	和	124
yawa(ragu)	和	124
yawa(raka)	柔	774
yawa(rakai)	柔	774
YO	与	539
	予	393
	預	394
yo	世	252
	夜	471
	代	256
	四	6
YŌ	容	654
	揚	631
	曜	19
	様	403
	洋	289
	用	107
	羊	288
	養	402
	葉	253
	要	419
	陽	630
yō	八	10
yogo(reru)	汚	693
yogo(su)	汚	693
yo(i)	良	321
YOKU	翌	592
yo(mu)	読	244
yon	四	6
yoru	夜	471
yo(ru)	因	554
yoshi	由	363
yo(tsu)	四	6
yot(tsu)	四	6
yowa(i)	弱	218
yowa(maru)	弱	218
yowa(meru)	弱	218
yowa(ru)	弱	218
YU	由	363
	油	364
	輸	546
yu	湯	632
YŪ	由	363
	友	264
	右	76
	有	265
	郵	524
	夕	81
yū	故	173
yue	由	363
YUI	由	363
yu(ku)	行	68
yumi	弓	212
yuru(su)	許	737
yu(u)	結	485
yu(waeru)	結	485

– Z –

Reading	Kanji	Page
ZAI	在	268
	材	552
	財	553
	剤	550
ZAN	残	650
ZATSU	雑	575
ZEI	税	399
	説	400
ZEN	全	89
	前	47
	然	651
zeni	銭	648
ZETSU	絶	742
ZŌ	像	740
	増	712
	象	739
	造	691
	雑	575
ZOKU	族	221
	続	243
ZON	存	269
ZU	事	80
	図	339
	頭	276